Blessings and Prayers for Men

A DEVOTIONAL COMPANION

*Blessings and Prayers for*

# MEN

CONCORDIA PUBLISHING HOUSE · SAINT LOUIS

# CONTENTS

# PREFACE

Prayer is a natural and common part of the Christian's conversation with God; a conversation He initiates in Word and Sacrament. The prayer of a Christian flows from the relationship forged by the Savior who, by His sacrifice on the cross, has given you access to the heart of God. Prayer is not merely a pious act, but a way to bring glory to God and tend to your and your neighbor's bodily and spiritual welfare.

The familiar words and rhythms selected for this devotional are drawn from the words often heard in worship as we gather in community. The goal of this little book is to be a convenient resource to inform and encourage you in your prayer life. Through regular use it can assist you in making your whole life one of communion with your gracious heavenly Father.

*Scot A. Kinnaman*

*Editor*

Let the words of my mouth and

the meditation of my heart

be acceptable in Your sight,

O LORD, my Rock and my Redeemer.

*Psalm 19:14*

These brief services are intended as a simple form of daily prayer for individuals, families, small groups, and other settings.

When more than one person is present, the versicles and responses may be spoken responsively, with one person reading the words in regular type and the others responding with the words in **bold type.** Prayers may be prayed in the same fashion, although those in bold type are to be prayed by all.

For the readings, several verses have been recommended for each particular time of day. These may be used on a rotating basis. The value in using these few texts lies in the opportunity to learn them well. For those desiring a more complete selection of readings, daily lectionaries, such as those found in a hymnal may be used. Meditations as well as readings from Luther's Small and Large Catechisms may be included.

In the "prayers for others and ourselves," the following suggestions are intended to establish a pattern of daily and weekly prayer.

**Sunday:** For the joy of the resurrection among us; for the fruit of faith nourished by the Word and the Sacraments.

**Monday:** For faith to live in the promises of Holy Baptism; for one's calling and daily work; for the unemployed; for the salvation and well-being of our neighbors; for schools, colleges, and seminaries; for good government and for peace.

**Tuesday:** For deliverance against temptation and evil; for the addicted and despairing, the tortured and oppressed; for those struggling with sin.

**Wednesday:** For marriage and family, that husbands and wives, parents and children live in ordered harmony according to the Word of God; for parents who must raise children alone; for those looking for a faithful spouse; for our communities and neighborhoods.

**Thursday:** For the Church and her pastors; for teachers, deacons and deaconesses, for missionaries, and for all who serve the Church; for fruitful and salutary use of the blessed Sacrament of Christ's body and blood.

**Friday:** For the preaching of the holy cross of our Lord Jesus Christ and for the spread of His knowledge throughout the whole world; for the persecuted and oppressed; for the sick and dying.

**Saturday:** For faithfulness to the end; for the renewal of those who are withering in the faith or have fallen away; for receptive hearts and minds to God's Word on the Lord's Day; for pastors and people as they prepare to administer and receive Christ's holy gifts.

# Morning

*The sign of the cross may be made by all in remembrance of their Baptism.*

In the name of the Father and of the ✠ Son and of the Holy Spirit.

**Amen.**

O LORD, in the morning You hear my voice;

**in the morning I prepare a sacrifice for You and watch.** *Psalm 5:3*

My mouth is filled with Your praise,

**and with Your glory all the day.** *Psalm 71:8*

O Lord, open my lips,

**and my mouth will declare Your praise.**

*Psalm 51:15*

**Glory be to the Father and to the Son and to the Holy Spirit; as it was in the beginning, is now, and will be forever. Amen.**

*A hymn, canticle, or psalm may be sung or spoken.*

*An appointed reading or one of the following is read: Colossians 3:1–4; Exodus 15:1–11; Isaiah 12:1–6; Matthew 20:1–16; Mark 13:32–36; Luke 24:1–8; John 21:4–14; Ephesians 4:17–24; Romans 6:1–4.*

*A meditation or selection from the catechism may be read.*

*The Apostles' Creed is confessed.*

*Lord's Prayer*

*Prayers for others and ourselves*

*Concluding prayers:*

Almighty God, merciful Father, who created and completed all things, on this day when the work of our calling begins anew, we implore You to create its beginning, direct its continuance, and bless its end, that our doings may be preserved from sin, our life sanctified, and our work this day be well pleasing to You; through Jesus Christ, our Lord. Amen.

**I thank You, my heavenly Father, through Jesus Christ, Your dear Son, that You have kept me this night from all harm and danger; and I pray that You would keep me this day also from sin and every evil, that all my doings and life may please You. For into Your hands I commend myself, my body and soul, and all things. Let Your holy angel be with me, that the evil foe may have no power over me. Amen.** (Luther's Morning Prayer, Small Catechism)

Let us bless the Lord.

**Thanks be to God.**

*Then go joyfully to your work.*

# Noon

*The sign of the cross may be made by all in remembrance of their Baptism.*

In the name of the Father and of the ✠ Son and of the Holy Spirit.

**Amen.**

Listen to my prayer, O God, do not ignore my plea;

**hear my prayer and answer me.**

Evening, morning, and noon

**I cry out in distress and He hears my voice.**

Cast your cares on the Lord and He will sustain you;

**He will never let the righteous fall.**

*Psalm 55:1, 16–17, 22*

**Glory be to the Father and to the Son and to the Holy Spirit; as it was in the beginning, is now, and will be forever. Amen.**

*A hymn, canticle, or psalm may be sung or said.*

*An appointed reading or one of the following is read: 1 Corinthians 7:17a, 23–24; Luke 23:44–46; Matthew 5:13–16; Matthew 13:1–9, 18–23; Mark 13:23–27; John 15:1–9; Romans 7:18–25; Romans*

*12:1–2; 1 Peter 1:3–9.*

O Lord,

**have mercy upon us.**

O Christ,

**have mercy upon us.**

O Lord,

**have mercy upon us.**

*Lord's Prayer*

*Prayers for others and ourselves*

*Concluding prayer:*

Blessed Lord Jesus Christ, at this hour You hung upon the cross, stretching out Your loving arms to embrace the world in Your death. Grant that all people of the earth may look to You and see their salvation; for your mercy's sake we pray. **Amen.**

*(OR)*

Heavenly Father, send Your Holy Spirit into our hearts, to direct and rule us according to Your will, to comfort us in all our afflictions, to defend us from all error, and to lead us into all truth; through Jesus Christ, our Lord. **Amen.**

Let us bless the Lord.

**Thanks be to God.**

# Early Evening

*The sign of the cross may be made by all in remembrance of their Baptism.*

In the name of the Father and of the ✠ Son and of the Holy Spirit.

**Amen.**

*A candle may be lighted.*

Let my prayer rise before You as incense;

**the lifting up of my hands as the evening sacrifice.** *Psalm 141:2*

**Joyous light of glory of the immortal Father; heavenly, holy, blessed Jesus Christ. We have come to the setting of the sun, and we look to the evening light. We sing to God, the Father, Son, and Holy Spirit: You are worthy of being praised with pure voices forever. O Son of God, O giver of life: the universe proclaims Your glory.**

*A hymn, canticle, or psalm may be sung or said.*

*An appointed reading or one of the following is read: Luke 24:28–31; Exodus 16:11–21, 31; Isaiah 25:6–9; Matthew 14:15–21; Matthew 27:57–60; Luke 14:15–24; John 6:25–35; John 10:7–18; Ephesians 6:10–18.*

*A meditation or selection from the catechism may be read.*

*Lord's Prayer*

*Prayers for others and ourselves*

*Concluding prayer:*

Lord Jesus, stay with us, for the evening is at hand and the day is past. Be our constant companion on the way, kindle our hearts, and awaken hope among us, that we may recognize You as You are revealed in the Scriptures and in the Breaking of the Bread. Grant this for Your name's sake. **Amen.**

Let us bless the Lord.

**Thanks be to God.**

Mealtime Prayers:

*Asking a blessing before the meal*

**Lord God, heavenly Father, bless us and these Your gifts which we receive from Your bountiful goodness, through Jesus Christ, our Lord. Amen.**

*Returning thanks after the meal*

**We thank You, Lord God, heavenly Father, through Jesus Christ, our Lord, for all Your benefits, who lives and reigns with You forever and ever. Amen.**

# Close of the Day

*The sign of the cross may be made by all in remembrance of their Baptism.*

In the name of the Father and of the ✠ Son and of the Holy Spirit.

**Amen.**

The Lord Almighty grant us a quiet night and peace at the last.

**Amen.**

It is good to give thanks to the Lord,

**to sing praise to Your name, O Most High;**

To herald Your love in the morning,

**Your truth at the close of the day.**

*An appointed reading or one of the following is read: Matthew 11:28–30; Micah 7:18–20; Matthew 18:15–35; Matthew 25:1–13; Luke 11:1–13; Luke 12:13–34; Romans 8:31–39; 2 Corinthians 4:16–18; Revelation 21:22–22:5.*

*The Apostles' Creed is confessed.*

**Lord, now You let Your servant go in peace; Your word has been fulfilled.**

**My own eyes have seen the salvation which You have prepared in the sight of every people:**

a light to lighten the nations and the glory of Your people Israel.                    *Luke 2:29–32*

Glory be to the Father and to the Son and to the Holy Spirit;

as it was in the beginning, is now, and will be forever. Amen.

*Lord's Prayer*

*Prayers for others and ourselves*

*Concluding prayers:*

Visit our dwellings, O Lord, and in Your great mercy defend us from all perils and dangers of this night; for the love of Your only Son, our Savior Jesus Christ. Amen.

I thank You, my heavenly Father, through Jesus Christ, Your dear Son, that You have graciously kept me this day; and I pray that You would forgive me all my sins where I have done wrong, and graciously keep me this night. For into Your hands I commend myself, my body and soul, and all things. Let Your holy angel be with me, that the evil foe may have no power over me. Amen. *(Luther's Evening Prayer, Small Catechism)*

Let us bless the Lord.

**Thanks be to God.**

*Then be at peace and rest in God's care.*

# Selection of Hymns

*The following selected hymns are appropriate for the festivals and times of the church:*

# A Mighty Fortress Is Our God

1. A mighty fortress is our God,
   A trusty shield and weapon;
   He helps us free from ev'ry need
   That hath us now o'ertaken.
   The old evil foe
   Now means deadly woe;
   Deep guile and great might
   Are his dread arms in fight;
   On earth is not his equal.

2. With might of ours can naught be done,
   Soon were our loss effected;
   But for us fights the valiant One,
   Whom God Himself elected.
   Ask ye, Who is this?
   Jesus Christ it is.
   Of Sabaoth Lord,
   And there's none other God;
   He holds the field forever.

3. Though devils all the world should fill,
   All eager to devour us,
   We tremble not, we fear no ill,
   They shall not overpower us.
   This world's prince may still
   Scowl fierce as he will,
   He can harm us none,
   He's judged; the deed is done;
   One little word can fell him.

4. The Word they still shall let remain
   Nor any thanks have for it;
   He's by our side upon the plain
   With his good gifts and Spirit.
   And take they our life,
   Goods, fame, child, and wife,
   Let these all be gone,
   They yet have nothing won;
   The Kingdom ours remaineth.          (*LW* 298)

   Text: Martin Luther

## Abide with Me

1. Abide with me, fast falls the eventide.
   The darkness deepens; Lord with me abide.
   When other helpers fail and comforts flee,
   Help of the helpless, oh, abide with me.

2. I need thy presence every passing hour;
   What but thy grace can foil the tempter's
   power?
   Who like thyself my guide and stay can be?
   Through cloud and sunshine, oh, abide with
   me.

3. Come not in terrors, as the King of Kings,
   But kind and good, with healing in thy wings
   Tears for all woes, a heart for every plea.
   Come, Friend of sinners, thus abide with me.

4. Swift to its close ebbs out life's little day;
   Earth's joys grow dim, its glories pass away;

Change and decay in all around I see.
O thou, who changest not, abide with me.

5. Thou on my head in early youth did smile,
And though rebellious and perverse
meanwhile,
Thou hast not left me, oft as I left thee.
On to the close, O Lord, abide with me.

6. I fear no foe, with thee at hand to bless;
Ills have no weight and tears no bitterness,
Where is death's sting? where, grave, thy
victory?
I triumph still if thou abide with me!

7. Hold thou thy cross before my closing eyes,
Shine through the gloom, and point me to
the skies.
Heav'n's morning breaks, and earth's vain
shadows flee;
In life, in death, O Lord, abide with me.

(*LW* 490:1–2,3–5, *TLH* 552:5)
Text: Henry F. Lyte

## All Praise to Thee, My God, This Night

1. All praise to thee, my God, this night
For all the blessings of the light.
Keep me, oh, keep me, King of kings,
Beneath thine own almighty wings.

2. Forgive me, Lord, for thy dear Son,
The ill that I this day have done;

That with the world, myself, and thee,
I, ere I sleep, at peace may be.

3. Teach me to live that I may dread
   The grave as little as my bed.
   Teach me to die that so I may
   Rise glorious at the awesome day.

4. Oh, may my soul in thee repose,
   And may sweet sleep mine eyelids close,
   Sleep that shall me more vigorous make
   To serve my God when I awake!

5. When in the night I sleepless lie,
   My soul with heav'nly thoughts supply;
   Let no ill dreams disturb my rest,
   No powers of darkness me molest.

6. Praise God, from whom all blessings flow,
   Praise him, all creatures here below;
   Praise him above, ye heav'nly host;
   Praise Father, Son, and Holy Ghost.
   (*LW* 484)
   Text: Thomas Ken

## All Christians Who Have Been Baptized

1. All Christians who have been baptized,
   Who know the God of heaven,
   And in whose daily life is prized
   The name of Christ once given;
   Consider now what God has done,
   The gifts He gives to ev'ryone
   Baptized into Christ Jesus.

2. You were before you day of birth,
   Indeed from your conception,
   Condemned and lost with all the earth,
   None good, without exception
   For like our parents' flesh and blood,
   Turned inward from the highest good,
   You constantly denied Him.

3. But all of that was washed away—
   Immersed and drowned forever
   The water of your Baptism day
   Restored again whatever
   Old Adam and his sin destroyed
   And all our sinful selves employed
   According to our nature.

4. In Baptism we now put on Christ—
   Our sin is fully covered
   With all that He once sacrificed
   And freely for us suffered.
   For here the flood of His own blood
   Now makes us holy, right and goodness
   Before our heav'nly Father.

5. O Christian, firmly hold this gift
   And give God thanks forever!
   It gives the power to uplift
   In all that you endeavor.
   When nothing else revives your soul,
   Your Baptism stands and makes you whole
   And then in death completes you.

6. So use it well! You are made new—

In Christ a new creation!
As faithful Christians, live and do
Within your own vocation,
Until that day when you possess
His glorious robe of righteousness
Bestowed on you forever!    (JV)

Text: Paul Gerhardt: tr. Jon Vieker

© 2004 Jon Vieker. Used with permission

## Be Still, My Soul

1. Be still, my soul; the Lord is on your side;
   Bear patiently the cross of grief or pain;
   Leave to your God to order and provide;
   In every change he faithful will remain.
   Be still, my soul; your best, your heavenly
   Friend
   Through thorny ways leads to a joyful end.

2. Be still, my soul; your God will undertake
   To guide the future as he has the past.
   Your hope, your confidence let nothing shake;
   All now mysterious shall be bright at last.
   Be still, my soul; the waves and wind still know
   His voice who ruled them while he dwelt below.

3. Be still, my soul; though dearest friends depart
   And all is darkened in the vale of tears;
   Then you will better know his love, his heart,
   Who comes to soothe your sorrows and
        your fears.
   Be still, my soul; your Jesus can repay

From his own fullness all he takes away.

4. Be still, my soul; the hour is hastening on
   When we shall be forever with the Lord,
   When disappointment, grief, and fear
       are gone,
   Sorrow forgot, love's purest joys restored.
   Be still, my soul; when change and tears
       are past,
   All safe and blessed we shall meet at last.
   *(LW 510)*

   Text: Catharina von Schlegel

## Chief of Sinners Though I Be

1. Chief of sinners though I be,
   Jesus shed his blood for me,
   Died that I might live on high,
   Lives that I might never die.
   As the branch is to the vine,
   I am his, and he is mine.

2. Oh, the height of Jesus' love,
   Higher than the heav'ns above,
   Deeper than the depths of sea,
   Lasting as eternity!
   Love that found me—wondrous thought—
   Found me when I sought him not.

3. Only Jesus can impart
   Balm to heal the wounded heart,
   Peace that flows from sin forgiv'n,

Joy that lifts the soul to heav'n,
Faith and hope to walk with God
In the way that Enoch trod.

4. Chief of sinners though I be,
Christ is all in all to me;
All my wants to him are known,
All my sorrows are his own.
He sustains the hidden life
Safe with him from earthly strife.

5. O my Savior, help afford
By your Spirit and your Word!
When my wayward heart would stray,
Keep me in the narrow way;
Grace in time of need supply
While I live and when I die.
*(LW 285)*

Text: William McComb

## For All the Saints Who from Their Labors Rest

1. For all the saints who from their labors rest,
Who Thee by faith before the world confest,
Thy name, O Jesus, be forever blest,
Alleluia! Alleluia!

2. Thou wast their Rock, their Fortress, and their
Might;
Thou, Lord, their Captain in the well-
fought fight;
Thou, in the darkness drear, their one true Light.
Alleluia! Alleluia!

3. Oh, may Thy soldiers, faithful, true and bold,
   Fight as the saints who nobly fought of old
   And win with them the victor's crown of gold.
   Alleluia! Alleluia!

4. O blest communion, fellowship divine,
   We feebly struggle, they in glory shine;
   Yet all are one in Thee, for all are Thine.
   Alleluia! Alleluia!

5. And when the fight is fierce, the warfare long,
   Steals on the ear the distant triumph song,
   And hearts are brave again, and arms
        are strong.
   Alleluia! Alleluia!

6. But, lo, there breaks a yet more glorious day;
   The saints triumphant rise in bright array;
   The King of Glory passes on His way.
   Alleluia! Alleluia!

7. The golden evening brightens in the west;
   Soon, soon, to faithful warriors cometh rest.
   Sweet is the calm of Paradise the blest.
   Alleluia! Alleluia!

8. From earth's wide bounds, from ocean's far-
   thest coast,
   Through gates of pearl streams in the
        countless host,
   Singing to Father, Son, and Holy Ghost,
   Alleluia! Alleluia!    (*TLH* 463)

Text: William W. How

# Glory Be to Jesus

1. Glory be to Jesus,
   Who in bitter pains
   Poured for me the lifeblood
   From his sacred veins.

2. Grace and life eternal
   In that blood I find;
   Blest be his compassion,
   Infinitely kind.

3. Blest through endless ages
   Be the precious stream
   Which from endless torment
   Did the world redeem.

4. Abel's blood for vengeance
   Pleaded to the skies;
   But the blood of Jesus
   For our pardon cries.

5. Oft as earth exulting
   Wafts its praise on high,
   Angel hosts rejoicing
   Make their glad reply.

6. Lift we then our voices,
   Swell the mighty flood;
   Louder still and louder
   Praise the precious blood.    (*LW* 98)

Text: Friedrich Filitz

# Holy, Holy, Holy

1. Holy, holy, holy, Lord God Almighty!
   Early in the morning our song shall
         rise to Thee.
   Holy, holy, holy, merciful and mighty!
   God in Three Persons, blessed Trinity!

2. Holy, holy, holy! All the saints adore Thee,
   Casting down their golden crowns around
         the glassy sea;
   Cherubim and seraphim falling down
         before Thee,
   Which wert and art and evermore shalt be.

3. Holy, holy, holy! Though the darkness
         hide Thee,
   Tho' the eyes of sinful man Thy glory
         may not see,
   Only Thou art holy; there is none beside Thee,
   Perfect in pow'r, in love, and purity.

4. Holy, holy, holy, Lord God Almighty!
   All Thy works shall praise Thy name in earth
         and sky and sea.
   Holy, holy, holy, merciful and mighty!
   God in Three Persons, blessed Trinity!
   (*TLH* 246)

Text: Reginald Heber

# If God Had Not Been on Our Side

1. If God had not been on our side

And had not come to aid us,
The foes with all their power and pride
Would surely have dismayed us;
For we, His flock, would have to fear
The threat of men both far and near
Who rise in might against us.

2. Their furious wrath, did God permit,
   Would surely have consumed us
   And as a deep and yawning pit
   With life and limb entombed us.
   Like men o'er whom dark waters roll
   Their wrath would have engulfed our soul
   And, like a flood, o'erwhelmed us.

3. Blest be the Lord, who foiled their threat
   That they could not devour us;
   Our souls, like birds, escaped their net,
   They could not overpower us.
   The snare is broken—we are free!
   Our help is ever, Lord, in Thee,
   Who madest earth and heaven.
   (*TLH* 267)

Text: Martin Luther

## Jesus Christ Is Risen Today

1. Jesus Christ is risen today, Alleluia!
   Our triumphant holy day, Alleluia!
   Who did once upon the cross, Alleluia!
   Suffer to redeem our loss. Alleluia!

2. Hymns of praise then let us sing, Alleluia!
   Unto Christ, our heavenly king, Alleluia!
   Who endured the cross and grave, Alleluia!
   Sinners to redeem and save. Alleluia!

3. But the pains which he endured, Alleluia!
   Our salvation have procured; Alleluia!
   Now above the sky he's king, Alleluia!
   Where the angels ever sing. Alleluia!

4. Sing we to our God above, Alleluia!
   Praise eternal as his love; Alleluia!
   Praise him, all you heavenly host, Alleluia!
   Father, Son, and Holy Ghost. Alleluia!
   (*LW* 127)

   Text: Latin Carol, sts. 1–3; Charles Wesley, st. 4

## Joy to the World

1. Joy to the world, the Lord is come!
   Let earth receive her King;
   Let ev'ry heart prepare Him room
   And heav'n and nature sing,
   And heav'n and nature sing,
   And heav'n, and heav'n and nature sing.

2. Joy to the earth, the Savior reigns!
   Let men their songs employ
   While fields and floods, rocks, hills, and
   plains
   Repeat the sounding joy,
   Repeat the sounding joy,

Repeat, repeat the sounding joy.

3. No more let sin and sorrows grow
   Nor thorns infest the ground;
   He comes to make His blessings flow
   Far as the curse is found,
   Far as the curse is found,
   Far as, far as the curse is found.

4. He rules the world with truth and grace
   And makes the nations prove
   The glories of His righteousness
   And wonders of His love,
   And wonders of His love,
   And wonders, wonders of His love. *(TLH 87)*

   Text: Isaac Watts

## O God, Thou Faithful God

1. O God, Thou faithful God,
   Thou Fountain ever flowing,
   Who good and perfect gifts
   In mercy art bestowing,
   Give me a healthy frame,
   And may I have within
   A conscience free from blame,
   A soul unhurt by sin!

2. Grant Thou me strength to do
   With ready heart and willing
   Whate'er Thou shalt command,
   My calling here fulfilling;
   To do it when I ought,

With all my might, and bless
The work I thus have wrought,
For Thou must give success.

3. Oh, let me never speak
What bounds of truth exceedth;
Grant that no idle word
From out my mouth proceedeth;
And then, when in my place
I must and ought to speak,
My words grant power and grace
Lest I offend the weak.

4. If dangers gather round,
Still keep me calm and fearless;
Help me to bear the cross
When life is dark and cheerless;
And let me win my foe
With words and actions kind.
When counsel I would know,
Good counsel let me find.

5. And let me with all men,
As far as in me lieth,
In peace and friendship live.
And if Thy gift supplieth
Great wealth and honor fair,
Then this refuse me not,
That naught be mingled there
Of goods unjustly got.

6. If Thou a longer life

Hast here on earth decreed me;
If Thou through many ills
To age at length wilt lead me;
Thy patience on me shed.
Avert all sin and shame
And crown my hoary head
With honor free from blame.

7. Let me depart this life
Confiding in my Savior;
Do Thou my soul receive
That it may live forever;
And let my body have
A quiet resting-place
Within a Christian grave;
And let it sleep in peace.

8. And on that solemn Day
When all the dead are waking,
Stretch o'er my grave Thy hand,
Thyself my slumber breaking.
Then let me hear Thy voice,
Change Thou this earthly frame,
And bid me aye rejoice
With those who love Thy name. (*TLH* 395)

Text: Johann Heermann

## Praise God, from Whom All Blessings Flow

Praise God, from whom all blessings flow;
Praise Him, all creatures here below;
Praise Him above, ye heav'nly host;

Praise Father, Son, and Holy Ghost. (*TLH* 644)

Text: Thomas Ken

## Savior of the Nations, Come

1. Savior of the nations, come,
   Virgin's Son, make here Thy home!
   Marvel now, O heaven and earth,
   That the Lord chose such a birth.

2. Not by human flesh and blood,
   By the Spirit of our God,
   Was the Word of God made flesh—
   Woman's Offspring, pure and fresh.

3. Here a maid was found with child,
   Virgin pure and undefiled.
   In her virtues it was known
   God had made her heart his throne.

4. Then stepped forth the Lord of all
   From his pure and kingly hall;
   God of God, becoming man,
   His heroic course began.

5. God the Father was his source,
   Back to God he ran his course.
   Into hell his road went down,
   Back then to his throne and crown.

6. Father's equal, you will win
   Vict'ries for us over sin.
   Might eternal, make us whole,
   Heal our ills of flesh and soul.

7. From the manger newborn light
   Shines in glory through the night.
   Night cannot this light subdue,
   Faith keeps springing ever new.

8. Glory to the Father sing,
   Glory to the Son, our king,
   Glory to the Spirit be
   Now and through eternity.
   (*TLH* 95:1,2, *LW* 13:3–8)
   Text: St. Ambrose

## Silent Night

1. Silent night! holy night!
   All is calm, all is bright
   Round yon virgin Mother and Child.
   Holy Infant, so tender and mild,
   Sleep in heavenly peace,
   Sleep in heavenly peace.

2. Silent night! holy night!
   Shepherds quake at the sight;
   Glories stream from heaven afar,
   Heav'nly hosts sing, Alleluia!
   Christ, the Savior, is born!
   Christ, the Savior, is born!

3. Silent night! holy night!
   Son of God, love's pure light
   Radiant beams from Thy holy face
   With the dawn of redeeming grace,

Jesus, Lord, at Thy birth,
Jesus, Lord, at Thy birth.    (*TLH* 646)

Text: Joseph Mohr

## Songs of Thankfulness and Praise

1. Songs of thankfulness and praise,
   Jesus, Lord, to Thee we raise,
   Manifested by the star
   To the sages from afar,
   Branch of royal David's stem,
   In Thy birth at Bethlehem.
   Anthems be to Thee addressed
   God in man made manifest.

2. Manifest at Jordan's stream,
   Prophet, Priest, and King supreme,
   And at Cana, Wedding-guest,
   In Thy Godhead manifest;
   Manifest in power divine,
   Changing water into wine.
   Anthems be to Thee addressed
   God in man made manifest.

3. Manifest in making whole
   Palsied limbs and fainting soul;
   Manifest in valiant fight,
   Quelling all the devil's might;
   Manifest in gracious will,
   Ever bringing good from ill.
   Anthems be to Thee addressed
   God in man made manifest.

4. Sun and moon shall darkened be,
   Stars shall fall, the heavens shall flee;
   Christ will then like lightning shine,
   All will see His glorious sign;
   All will then the trumpet hear,
   All will see the Judge appear;
   Thou by all wilt be confessed,
   God in man made manifest.

5. Grant us grace to see Thee, Lord,
   Present in Thy holy Word;
   Grace to imitate Thee now
   And be pure as pure art Thou
   That we might become like Thee.
   At Thy great Epiphany
   And may praise Thee, ever blest,
   God in man made manifest. (*TLH* 134)

Text : Christopher Wordsworth

## The Lord's My Shepherd, I'll Not Want

1. The Lord's my shepherd, I'll not want;
   He makes me down to lie
   In pastures green; He leadeth me
   The quiet waters by.

2. My soul he doth restore again
   And me to walk doth make
   Within the paths of righteousness,
   Even for his own name's sake.

3. Yea, though I walk in death's dark vale,

Yet will I fear no ill;
For thou art with me, and thy rod
And staff me comfort still.

4. My table thou hast furnished
In presence of my foes;
My head thou dost with oil anoint,
And my cup overflows.

5. Goodness and mercy all my life
Shall surely follow me;
And in God's house forevermore
My dwelling place shall be. (*LW* 416)

Text: William Gardiner

## The Man Is Ever Blest

1. The man is ever blessed
Who shuns the sinners' ways,
Among their counsels never stands,
Nor takes the scorners' place.

2. But makes the Law of God
His study and delight
Amid the labors of the day
And watches of the night.

3. He like a tree shall thrive,
With waters near the root;
Fresh as the leaf his name shall live,
His works are heavenly fruit.

4. Not so the wicked race,

They no such blessings find;
Their hopes shall flee like empty chaff
Before the driving wind.

5. How will they bear to stand
Before the judgment seat
Where all the saints at Christ's right hand
In full assembly meet?

6. He knows and he approves
The way the righteous go;
But sinners and their works shall meet
A dreadful overthrow.        (*LW* 388)

Text: Isaac Watts

## Thy Strong Word

1. Thy strong word did cleave the darkness;
At thy speaking it was done.
For created light we thank thee,
While thine ordered seasons run.
Alleluia, alleluia!
Praise to thee who light dost send!
Alleluia, alleluia!
Alleluia without end!

2. Lo, on those who dwelt in darkness,
Dark as night and deep as death,
Broke the light of thy salvation,
Breathed thine own life-breathing breath.
Alleluia, alleluia!
Praise to thee who light dost send!

Alleluia, alleluia!
Alleluia without end!

3. Thy strong Word bespeaks us righteous;
   Bright with thine own holiness,
   Glorious now, we press toward glory,
   And our lives our hopes confess.
   Alleluia, alleluia!
   Praise to thee who light dost send!
   Alleluia, alleluia!
   Alleluia without end!

4. From the cross thy wisdom shining
   Breaketh forth in conqu'ring might;
   From the cross forever beameth
   All thy bright redeeming light.
   Alleluia, alleluia!
   Praise to thee who light dost send!
   Alleluia, alleluia!
   Alleluia without end!

5. Give us lips to sing thy glory,
   Tongues thy mercy to proclaim
   Throats that shout the hope that fills us,
   Mouths to speak thy holy name.
   Alleluia, alleluia!
   May the light which thou dost send
   Fill our songs with alleluias,
   Alleluia without end!

6. God the Father, light-creator,
   To thee laud and honor be.
   To thee, Light of Light begotten,

Praise be sung eternally.
Holy Spirit, light-revealer,
Glory, glory be to thee.
Mortals, angels, now and ever
Praise the holy Trinity!     *(LW 328)*

Text: Martin H. Franzmann

## We All Believe in One True God, Father

1. We all believe in one true God,
   Father, Son, and Holy Ghost,
   Ever-present help in need,
   Praised by all the heavenly host;
   All he made his love enfolds,
   All creation he upholds.

2. We all believe in Jesus Christ,
   Son of God and Mary's son,
   Who descended from his throne
   And for us salvation won;
   By whose cross and death are we
   Rescued from all misery.

3. We all confess the Holy Ghost,
   Who from both in truth proceeds,
   Who sustains and comforts us
   In all trials, fears, and needs.
   Blest and holy Trinity,
   Praise forever yours shall be. *(LW 212)*

Text: Tobias Clausnitzer

# With the Lord Begin Your Task

1. With the Lord begin your task;
   Jesus will direct it.
   For his aid and counsel ask;
   Jesus will perfect it.
   Every morn with Jesus rise,
   And when day is ended,
   In his name then close your eyes;
   Be to him commended.

2. Let each day begin with prayer,
   Praise, and adoration.
   On the Lord cast every care;
   He is your salvation.
   Morning, evening, and at night
   Jesus will be near you,
   Save you from the tempter's might,
   With his presence cheer you.

3. With the Savior at your side,
   Foes need not alarm you;
   In His promises confide,
   And no ill can harm you.
   All your trust and hope repose
   In the mighty Master,
   Who in wisdom truly knows
   How to stem disaster.

4. If your task be thus begun
   With the Savior's blessing,
   Safely then your course will run,
   Toward the promise pressing.

Good will follow ev'rywhere
While you here must wander.
You at last the joy will share
In the mansions yonder. (*LW* 483)

Text: Moren-und Abend-segen, Waldenburg

# Selection of Canticles

## The Benedictus (Zechariah's Song)

Blessed be the Lord God of Israel; for He has visited and redeemed His people and has raised up a horn of salvation for us in the house of His servant David, as He spoke by the mouth of His holy prophets, who have been since the world began. That we should be saved from our enemies and from the hand of all who hate us; to perform the mercy promised to our fathers and remember His holy covenant, the oath that He swore to our father Abraham, to grant us that we, being delivered from the hand of our enemies, might serve Him without fear, in holiness and righteousness before Him all the days of our life.

*[During Advent:]* And You, child, will be called the prophet of the Most High; for You will go before the Lord to prepare His ways, to give knowledge of salvation to His people in the forgiveness of their sins, through the tender mercy of our God; when the day shall dawn upon us from on high to give light to them who sit in darkness and in the shadow of death, to guide our feet in the way of peace.

## Nunc dimittis (Simeon's Song)

Lord, now let Your servant depart in peace according to Your word, for my eyes have seen Your salvation, which You have prepared before the face of all people, a Light to lighten the Gentiles, and the glory of Your people Israel.

Glory be to the Father and to the Son and to the Holy Ghost; as it was in the beginning, is now and ever shall be, world without end. Amen.

## Te Deum laudamus

We praise You, O God; we acknowledge You to be the Lord; all the earth now worships You, the Father everlasting. To You all angels cry aloud, the heavens and all the powers therein.

To You cherubim and seraphim continually do cry: Holy, holy, holy, Lord God of Sabaoth; heaven and earth are full of the majesty of Your glory. The glorious company of the apostles praise You; the goodly fellowship of the prophets praise You. The noble army of martyrs praise You. The holy Church throughout all the world does acknowledge You: The Father of an infinite majesty; Your adorable true and only Son, also the Holy Ghost, the comforter. You are the King of glory, O Christ; You are the everlasting Son of the Father.

When You took upon Yourself to deliver man,

You humbled Yourself to be born of a virgin. When You had overcome the sharpness of death, You opened the kingdom of heaven to all believers. You sit at the right hand of God in the glory of the Father. We believe that You will come to be our judge.

We therefore pray You to help Your servants, whom You have redeemed with Your precious blood. Make them to be numbered with Your saints in glory everlasting.

O Lord, save Your people and bless Your heritage. Govern them and lift them up forever. Day by day we magnify You. And we worship Your name ever, world without end. Vouchsafe, O Lord, to keep us this day without sin. O Lord, have mercy upon us, have mercy upon us. O Lord, let Your mercy be upon us, as our trust is in You. O Lord, in You have I trusted; let me never be confounded.

## The Magnificat (Mary's Song)

My soul magnifies the Lord, and my spirit rejoices in God, my Savior; for He has regarded the lowliness of His handmaiden. For, behold, from this day all generations will call me blessed. For the Mighty One has done great things to me, and Holy is His name; and His mercy is on those who fear Him from generation to generation. He has shown strength with His arm; He has scattered the proud in the imagination of their hearts. He has cast down the mighty from their thrones, and has exalted the lowly. He has filled the hungry with good things, and the rich He has sent away empty. He has helped His servant Israel in remembrance of His mercy, as He spoke to our fathers, to Abraham, and to his seed forever.

# Selection of Psalms

## Themes in the Selected Psalms

Assurance—119:9–16; 121

Close of Day—16:1–5, 10–14

Confession—51

Consolation and Comfort—38:9, 21–22; 90

Danger—143

Evening—46

Forgiveness—32, 119:33–46

Marriage—127

Mercy—6, 130:1–6, 142

Morning—100

Penitential Psalms—6, 32, 38, 51, 102, 130, 143

Praise—30, 138

Righteousness—1

Trouble—6, 38, 102

Trust—23, 130

# Other Psalms for Daily Prayer

## Suggested for Devotional Reading:

### Morning Prayer
Sundays and Festivals: 1, 2, 8, 19, 27, 45, 62, 67, 72, 84, 98

Other Days: 5, 18, 22, 24, 25, 28, 50, 65, 73, 92, 96, 100, 107, 119, 147, 148

### Evening Prayer
Sundays and Festivals: 23, 110, 111, 114
Other Days: 38, 51, 105, 116, 117, 118, 126, 130, 135, 136, 138, 139, 141, 143, 146

### Close of the Day
Sundays and Festivals: 91, 133, 134

Other Days: 4, 12, 34, 77, 103

## Themes in Christian Life

Affliction: 34, 130
Comfort: 116, 118
Confession: 30, 102
Confidence and Trust: 16, 25, 27, 37, 62, 91, 121, 139
Encouragement: 73
Eternal Life: 16, 17, 49, 116
Forgiveness: 103
Marriage: 45, 127
Mercy: 6, 25, 32, 36, 38, 73, 77, 102, 143
Praise: 9, 18, 32, 40, 66, 92, 98, 100, 116, 145
Prayer: 17, 86, 90, 102, 142
Thanksgiving: 30, 31, 100, 116, 124, 126, 136
Trust: 27, 62, 63, 71, 131
Salvation: 40, 67, 128
Strength in the Face of Tribulation: 3, 5, 10, 43, 54, 57, 77

## ❦Righteousness                    Psalm 1

Blessed is the man
    who walks not in the counsel of the wicked,
nor stands in the way of sinners,
    nor sits in the seat of scoffers;
²but his delight is in the law of the LORD,
    and on His law he meditates day and night.
³He is like a tree
    planted by streams of water
that yields its fruit in its season,
    and its leaf does not wither.
In all that he does, he prospers.
⁴The wicked are not so,
    but are like chaff that the wind drives away.
⁵Therefore the wicked will not stand in the
        judgment,
    nor sinners in the congregation of the
        righteous;
⁶for the LORD knows the way of the righteous,
    but the way of the wicked will perish.

## ❦In Time of Trouble               Psalm 6

O LORD, rebuke me not in Your anger,
    nor discipline me in Your wrath.
²Be gracious to me, O LORD, for I am languish-
ing;

heal me, O Lord, for my bones are troubled.
³My soul also is greatly troubled.

But You, O Lord—how long?
⁴Turn, O Lord, deliver my life;

save me for the sake of Your steadfast love.
⁵For in death there is no remembrance of You;

in Sheol who will give You praise?
⁶I am weary with my moaning;

every night I flood my bed with tears;

I drench my couch with my weeping.
⁷My eye wastes away because of grief;

it grows weak because of all my foes.
⁸Depart from me, all you workers of evil,

for the Lord has heard the sound of my
weeping.
⁹The Lord has heard my plea;

the Lord accepts my prayer.
¹⁰All my enemies shall be ashamed and greatly
troubled;

they shall turn back and be put to shame in
a moment.

## ✒ *Close of Day*                    Psalm 16:1–5, 10–11

Preserve me, O God, for in You I take refuge.
²I say to the Lord, "You are my Lord;

I have no good apart from You."
³As for the saints in the land, they are the

excellent ones,

in whom is all my delight.

⁴The sorrows of those who run after another
god shall multiply;

their drink offerings of blood I will not
pour out

or take their names on my lips.

⁵The LORD is my chosen portion and my cup;

You hold my lot. ...

¹⁰For You will not abandon my soul to Sheol,

or let Your holy one see corruption.

¹¹You make known to me the path of life;

in Your presence there is fullness of joy;

at Your right hand are pleasures forever
more.

## Trust                                    *Psalm 23*

The LORD is my shepherd; I shall not want.

²He makes me lie down in green pastures.

He leads me beside still waters.

³He restores my soul.

He leads me in paths of righteousness
for His name's sake.

⁴Even though I walk through the valley of the
shadow of death,

I will fear no evil,

for You are with me;

Your rod and your staff,
they comfort me.
⁵You prepare a table before me
in the presence of my enemies;
You anoint my head with oil;
my cup overflows.
⁶Surely goodness and mercy shall follow me
all the days of my life,
and I shall dwell in the house of the LORD
forever.

## ℘ *Praise*                            Psalm 30

I will extol You, O LORD, for You have drawn me up
and have not let my foes rejoice over me.
²O LORD my God, I cried to You for help,
and You have healed me.
³O LORD, You have brought up my soul from
Sheol;
You restored me to life from among those
who go down to the pit.
⁴Sing praises to the LORD, O You His saints,
and give thanks to His holy name.
⁵For His anger is but for a moment,
and His favor is for a lifetime.
Weeping may tarry for the night,
but joy comes with the morning.

⁶As for me, I said in my prosperity,
"I shall never be moved."
⁷By Your favor, O LORD,
You made my mountain stand strong;
You hid Your face;
I was dismayed.
⁸To You, O LORD, I cry,
and to the LORD I plead for mercy:
⁹"What profit is there in my death,
if I go down to the pit?
Will the dust praise You?
Will it tell of Your faithfulness?
¹⁰Hear, O LORD, and be merciful to me!
O LORD, be my helper!"
¹¹You have turned for me my mourning into
dancing;
You have loosed my sackcloth
and clothed me with gladness,
¹²that my glory may sing Your praise and
not be silent.
O LORD my God, I will give thanks to
You forever!

# ♫ Joy of Forgiveness                    Psalm 32

Blessed is the one whose transgression is forgiven,
whose sin is covered.
²Blessed is the man against whom the LORD

counts no iniquity,

and in whose spirit there is no deceit.

3For when I kept silent, my bones wasted away

through my groaning all day long.

4For day and night Your hand was heavy
upon me;

my strength was dried up as by the heat of
summer. *Selah*

5I acknowledged my sin to You,

and I did not cover my iniquity;

I said, "I will confess my transgressions
to the LORD,"

and You forgave the iniquity of my sin.
*Selah*

6Therefore let everyone who is godly

offer prayer to You at a time when You
may be found;

surely in the rush of great waters,

they shall not reach him.

7You are a hiding place for me;

You preserve me from trouble;

You surround me with shouts of deliverance.
*Selah*

8I will instruct you and teach you in the way
you should go;

I will counsel you with My eye upon you.

9Be not like a horse or a mule, without understanding,

which must be curbed with bit and bridle,
or it will not stay near you.
[10]Many are the sorrows of the wicked,
but steadfast love surrounds the one who
trusts in the LORD.
[11]Be glad in the LORD, and rejoice, O righteous,
and shout for joy, all you upright in heart!

## Consolation and Comfort          Psalm 38

O LORD, rebuke me not in Your anger,
nor discipline me in Your wrath!
[2]For Your arrows have sunk into me,
and Your hand has come down on me.
[3]There is no soundness in my flesh
because of Your indignation;
there is no health in my bones
because of my sin.
[4]For my iniquities have gone over my head;
like a heavy burden, they are too heavy
for me.
[5]My wounds stink and fester
because of my foolishness,
[6]I am utterly bowed down and prostrate;
all the day I go about mourning.
[7]For my sides are filled with burning,
and there is no soundness in my flesh.
[8]I am feeble and crushed;

I groan because of the tumult of my heart.

⁹O Lord, all my longing is before You;

my sighing is not hidden from You.

¹⁰My heart throbs; my strength fails me,

and the light of my eyes—it also has gone from me.

¹¹My friends and companions stand aloof from my plague,

and my nearest kin stand far off.

¹²Those who seek my life lay their snares;

those who seek my hurt speak of ruin

and meditate treachery all day long.

¹³But I am like a deaf man; I do not hear,

like a mute man who does not open his mouth.

¹⁴I have become like a man who does not hear,

and in whose mouth are no rebukes.

¹⁵But for You, O LORD, do I wait;

it is You, O Lord my God, who will answer.

¹⁶For I said, "Only let them not rejoice over me,

who boast against me when my foot slips!"

¹⁷For I am ready to fall,

and my pain is ever before me.

¹⁸I confess my iniquity;

I am sorry for my sin.

¹⁹But my foes are vigorous, they are mighty,

and many are those who hate me
wrongfully.

²⁰Those who render me evil for good

accuse me because I follow after good.

²¹Do not forsake me, O Lord!

O my God, be not far from me!

²²Make haste to help me,

O Lord, my salvation!

## ℰ *Evening*                    Psalm 46

God is our refuge and strength,

a very present help in trouble.

²Therefore we will not fear though the earth
gives way,

though the mountains be moved into
the heart of the sea,

³though its waters roar and foam,

though the mountains tremble at its
swelling. *Selah*

⁴There is a river whose streams make glad the
city of God,

the holy habitation of the Most High.

⁵God is in the midst of her; she shall not be
moved;

God will help her when morning dawns.

⁶The nations rage, the kingdoms totter;

He utters His voice, the earth melts.

7The LORD of hosts is with us;

　　the God of Jacob is our fortress. *Selah*

8Come, behold the works of the LORD,

　　how He has brought desolations on the
　　　　earth.

9He makes wars cease to the end of the earth;

　　He breaks the bow and shatters the spear;

　　He burns the chariots with fire.

10"Be still, and know that I am God.

　　I will be exalted among the nations,

　　I will be exalted in the earth!"

11The LORD of hosts is with us;

　　the God of Jacob is our fortress.

## ℘ *Prayer for Forgiveness - Confession*

### Psalm 51

Have mercy on me, O God,

　　according to Your steadfast love;

according to Your abundant mercy

　　blot out my transgressions.

2Wash me thoroughly from my iniquity,

　　and cleanse me from my sin!

3For I know my transgressions,

　　and my sin is ever before me.

4Against You, You only, have I sinned

　　and done what is evil in Your sight,

　　　　so that You may be justified in Your words

and blameless in Your judgment.
5Behold, I was brought forth in iniquity,
    and in sin did my mother conceive me.
6Behold, You delight in truth in the inward
        being,
    and You teach me wisdom in the secret
        heart.
7Purge me with hyssop, and I shall be clean;
    wash me, and I shall be whiter than snow.
8Let me hear joy and gladness;
    let the bones that You have broken rejoice.
9Hide Your face from my sins,
    and blot out all my iniquities.
10Create in me a clean heart, O God,
    and renew a right spirit within me.
11Cast me not away from Your presence,
    and take not Your Holy Spirit from me.
12Restore to me the joy of Your salvation,
    and uphold me with a willing spirit.
13Then I will teach transgressors Your ways,
    and sinners will return to You.
14Deliver me from bloodguiltiness, O God,
        O God of my salvation,
    and my tongue will sing aloud of Your righ-
        teousness.
15O Lord, open my lips,
    and my mouth will declare Your praise.

· ¹⁶For You will not delight in sacrifice, or I
would give it;

You will not be pleased with a burnt
offering.

¹⁷The sacrifices of God are a broken spirit;

a broken and contrite heart, O God, You
will not despise.

¹⁸Do good to Zion in Your good pleasure;

build up the walls of Jerusalem;

¹⁹then will You delight in right sacrifices,

in burnt offerings and whole burnt
offerings;

then bulls will be offered on Your altar.

## ❧Consolation and Comfort          Psalm 90

Lord, You have been our dwelling place
in all generations.

²Before the mountains were brought forth,

or ever You had formed the earth and the
world,

from everlasting to everlasting You are God.

³You return man to dust

and say, "Return, O children of man!"

⁴For a thousand years in Your sight

are but as yesterday when it is past,

or as a watch in the night.

⁵You sweep them away as with a flood; they are

like a dream,
like grass that is renewed in the morning:
⁶in the morning it flourishes and is renewed;
in the evening it fades and withers.
⁷For we are brought to an end by Your anger;
by Your wrath we are dismayed.
⁸You have set our iniquities before You,
our secret sins in the light of Your presence.
⁹For all our days pass away under Your wrath;
we bring our years to an end like a sigh.
¹⁰The years of our life are seventy,
or even by reason of strength eighty;
yet their span is but toil and trouble;
they are soon gone, and we fly away.
¹¹Who considers the power of Your anger,
and Your wrath according to the fear of
you?
¹²So teach us to number our days
that we may get a heart of wisdom.
¹³Return, O Lᴏʀᴅ! How long?
Have pity on Your servants!
¹⁴Satisfy us in the morning with Your steadfast
love,
that we may rejoice and be glad all our
days.
¹⁵Make us glad for as many days as You
have afflicted us,

and for as many years as we have seen evil.
¹⁶Let Your work be shown to Your servants,
    and Your glorious power to their children.

¹⁷Let the favor of the Lord our God be upon us
    and establish the work of our hands upon us;
    yes, establish the work of our hands!

## ✒ *Morning*                              Psalm 100

Make a joyful noise to the LORD, all the earth!
²Serve the LORD with gladness!
    Come into His presence with singing!
³Know that the LORD, He is God!
    It is He who made us, and we are His;
    we are His people, and the sheep of His
        pasture.
⁴Enter His gates with thanksgiving,
    and His courts with praise!
    Give thanks to Him; bless His name!
⁵For the LORD is good;
    His steadfast love endures forever,
    and His faithfulness to all generations.

## ✒ *In Times of Trouble*                    Psalm 102

Hear my prayer, O LORD;
let my cry come to You!

²Do not hide Your face from me
   in the day of my distress!
Incline Your ear to me;
   answer me speedily in the day when I call!

³For my days pass away like smoke,
   and my bones burn like a furnace.
⁴My heart is struck down like grass and has
   withered;
   I forget to eat my bread.
⁵Because of my loud groaning
   my bones cling to my flesh.
⁶I am like a desert owl of the wilderness,
   like an owl of the waste places;
⁷I lie awake;
   I am like a lonely sparrow on the housetop.
⁸All the day my enemies taunt me;
   those who deride me use my name for
   a curse.
⁹For I eat ashes like bread
   and mingle tears with my drink,
¹⁰because of Your indignation and anger;
   for You have taken me up and thrown
   me down.
¹¹My days are like an evening shadow;
   I wither away like grass.
¹²But You, O LORD, are enthroned forever;

You are remembered throughout all
generations.
¹³You will arise and have pity on Zion;
it is the time to favor her;
the appointed time has come.
¹⁴For Your servants hold her stones dear
and have pity on her dust.
¹⁵Nations will fear the name of the LORD,
and all the kings of the earth will fear
Your glory.
¹⁶For the LORD builds up Zion;
He appears in His glory;
¹⁷He regards the prayer of the destitute
and does not despise their prayer.
¹⁸Let this be recorded for a generation to come,
so that a people yet to be created may
praise the LORD:
¹⁹that He looked down from His holy height;
from heaven the LORD looked at the earth,
²⁰to hear the groans of the prisoners,
to set free those who were doomed to die,

²¹that they may declare in Zion the name
of the LORD,
and in Jerusalem His praise,
²²when peoples gather together,
and kingdoms, to worship the LORD.
²³He has broken my strength in midcourse;

He has shortened my days.
²⁴ "O my God," I say, "take me not away
in the midst of my days—
You whose years endure
throughout all generations!"
²⁵Of old You laid the foundation of the earth,
and the heavens are the work of Your
hands.
²⁶They will perish, but You will remain;
they will all wear out like a garment.
You will change them like a robe, and they
will pass away,
²⁷but You are the same, and Your years
have no end.
²⁸The children of Your servants shall dwell
secure;
their offspring shall be established before
You.

## Assurance                    Psalm 119:9–16

How can a young man keep his way pure?
By guarding it according to Your word.
¹⁰With my whole heart I seek You;
let me not wander from Your commandments!
¹¹I have stored up Your word in my heart,
that I might not sin against You.

[12]Blessed are You, O LORD;
   teach me Your statutes!
[13]With my lips I declare
   all the rules of Your mouth.
[14]In the way of Your testimonies I delight
   as much as in all riches.
[15]I will meditate on Your precepts
   and fix my eyes on Your ways.
[16]I will delight in Your statutes;
   I will not forget Your word.

## *Forgiveness*                        Psalm 119:33–46

Teach me, O LORD, the way of Your statutes;
   and I will keep it to the end.
[34]Give me understanding, that I may keep
      Your law
   and observe it with my whole heart.
[35]Lead me in the path of Your commandments,
   for I delight in it.
[36]Incline my heart to Your testimonies,
   and not to selfish gain!
[37]Turn my eyes from looking at worthless things;
   and give me life in Your ways.
[38]Confirm to Your servant Your promise,
   that You may be feared.
[39]Turn away the reproach that I dread,
   for Your rules are good.

⁴⁰Behold, I long for Your precepts;
   in Your righteousness give me life!
⁴¹Let Your steadfast love come to me, O LORD,
   Your salvation according to Your promise;
⁴²then shall I have an answer for him who
      taunts me,
   for I trust in Your word.
⁴³And take not the word of truth utterly out of
   my mouth,
   for my hope is in Your rules.
⁴⁴I will keep Your law continually,
   forever and ever,
⁴⁵and I shall walk in a wide place,
   for I have sought Your precepts.
⁴⁶I will also speak of Your testimonies before
   kings
   and shall not be put to shame,

## Assurance                    Psalm 121

I lift up my eyes to the hills.
   From where does my help come?
²My help comes from the LORD,
   who made heaven and earth.
³He will not let your foot be moved;
   He who keeps you will not slumber.
⁴Behold, He who keeps Israel
   will neither slumber nor sleep.

[5]The LORD is your keeper;
    the LORD is your shade on your right hand.
[6]The sun shall not strike you by day,
    nor the moon by night.
[7]The LORD will keep you from all evil;
    He will keep your life.
[8]The LORD will keep
    your going out and your coming in
    from this time forth and forevermore.

## Marriage                Psalm 127

Unless the LORD builds the house,
    those who build it labor in vain.
Unless the LORD watches over the city,
    the watchman stays awake in vain.
[2]It is in vain that you rise up early
    and go late to rest,
eating the bread of anxious toil;
    for He gives to His beloved sleep.
[3]Behold, children are a heritage from the LORD,
    the fruit of the womb a reward.
[4]Like arrows in the hand of a warrior
    are the children of one's youth.
[5]Blessed is the man
    who fills his quiver with them!
He shall not be put to shame

when he speaks with his enemies in
the gate.

## ✝ *Trust in God's Mercy*                    Psalm 130:1–6

Out of the depths I cry to You, O LORD!
²O LORD, hear my voice!
    Let your ears be attentive
    to the voice of my pleas for mercy!
³If You, O LORD, should mark iniquities,
    O Lord, who could stand?
⁴But with You there is forgiveness,
    that You may be feared.
⁵I wait for the LORD, my soul waits,
    and in His word I hope;
⁶my soul waits for the LORD
    more than watchmen for the morning,
    more than watchmen for the morning.

## ✝ *Mealtime, Returning Thanks*

Psalm 136:1, 25

¹Give thanks to the LORD, for He is good,
    for His steadfast love endures forever.
²⁵He gives food to all flesh,
    for His steadfast love endures forever.

## ✝ *Praise*                                         Psalm 138

I give You thanks, O LORD, with my whole heart;

before the gods I sing Your praise;
²I bow down toward Your holy temple
   and give thanks to Your name for Your
      steadfast love and Your faithfulness,
   for You have exalted above all things
   Your name and Your word.
³On the day I called, You answered me;
   my strength of soul You increased.
⁴All the kings of the earth shall give You thanks,
      O LORD,
   for they have heard the words of Your
      mouth,
⁵and they shall sing of the ways of the LORD,
   for great is the glory of the LORD.
⁶For though the LORD is high, He regards
      the lowly,
   but the haughty He knows from afar.
⁷Though I walk in the midst of trouble,
   You preserve my life;
You stretch out Your hand against the
      wrath of my enemies,
   and Your right hand delivers me.
⁸The LORD will fulfill His purpose for me;
   Your steadfast love, O LORD, endures forever.
   Do not forsake the work of Your hands.

# Mercy

With my voice I cry out to the LORD;

with my voice I plead for mercy to the LORD.

²I pour out my complaint before Him;

I tell my trouble before Him.

³When my spirit faints within me,

You know my way!

In the path where I walk

they have hidden a trap for me.

⁴Look to the right and see:

there is none who takes notice of me;

no refuge remains to me;

no one cares for my soul.

⁵I cry to You, O LORD;

I say, "You are my refuge,

my portion in the land of the living."

⁶Attend to my cry,

for I am brought very low!

Deliver me from my persecutors,

for they are too strong for me!

⁷Bring me out of prison,

that I may give thanks to Your name!

The righteous will surround me,

for You will deal bountifully with me.

# In Time of Danger

Hear my prayer, O LORD;

> give ear to my pleas for mercy!

In Your faithfulness answer me, in Your
righteousness!

²Enter not into judgment with Your servant,

> for no one living is righteous before You.

³For the enemy has pursued my soul;

> he has crushed my life to the ground;

> he has made me sit in darkness like those
long dead.

⁴Therefore my spirit faints within me;

> my heart within me is appalled.

⁵I remember the days of old;

> I meditate on all that You have done;

> I ponder the work of Your hands.

⁶I stretch out my hands to You;

> my soul thirsts for You like a parched land.
*Selah*

⁷Answer me quickly, O LORD!

> My spirit fails!

Hide not Your face from me,

> lest I be like those who go down to the pit.

⁸Let me hear in the morning of Your steadfast
love,

> for in You I trust.

Make me know the way I should go,
　　for to You I lift up my soul.
⁹Deliver me from my enemies, O Lord!
　　I have fled to You for refuge!
¹⁰Teach me to do Your will,
　　for You are my God!
Let your good Spirit lead me
　　on level ground!
¹¹For Your name's sake, O Lord, preserve my life!
　　In Your righteousness bring my soul out of
　　trouble!
¹²And in Your steadfast love You will cut off my
　　enemies,
　　and You will destroy all the adversaries of
　　my soul,
　　for I am Your servant.

# Selection of Scripture Lessons

*The selection of Scripture Lessons are arranged according to their order in the Bible.*

*The following are suggested for devotional readings and themes in Christian life:*

## Suggested for Devotional Reading:

### Morning:
Colossians 3:1–4;
Exodus 15:1–11;
Isaiah 12:1–6;
Matthew 20:1–16;
Mark 13:32–36;
Luke 24:1–8;
John 21:4–14;
Ephesians 4:17–24;
Romans 6:1–4.

### Noon:
1 Corinthians 7:17a, 23–24;
Luke 23:44–46;
Matthew 5:13–16;
Matthew 13:1–9, 18–23;
Mark 13:23–27;
John 15:1–9;
Romans 7:18–25;
Romans 12:1–2;
1 Peter 1:3–9.

### Early Evening:
Luke 24:28–31;
Exodus 16:11–21, 31;
Isaiah 25:6–9;
Matthew 14:15–21;
Matthew 27:57–60;
Luke 14:15–24;
John 6:25–35;
John 10:7–18;
Ephesians 6:10–18.

### Close of Day:
Matthew 11:28–30;
Micah 7:18–20;
Matthew 18:15–35;
Matthew 25:1–13;
Luke 11:1–13;
Luke 12:13–34;
Romans 8:31–39;
2 Corinthians 4:16–18;
Revelation 21:22–22:5.

## Church Year

**The Birth of Jesus:**
Luke 2:1–20

**The Death and Burial of Jesus:**
John 19:16–42

**The Resurrection of Jesus:**
Luke 24:1–8

## Themes in Christian Life

**Assurance:**
Job 19:21–27;
Psalm 139:1–6;

Micah 7:18–20;
Isaiah 43:1–3;
Romans 8:31–39;
Colossians 3:1–4;
1 John 3:1–2
**Children:**
Deuteronomy 6:4–7;
Matthew 18:2–6:
Ephesians 6:4
**Christian Life:**
Matthew 25:1-13;
Romans 6:1–4;
Ephesians 5:1–4;
Jude 20–25
**Confidence:**
Hebrews 10:35–36;
Hebrews 12:1–11;
1 Peter 1:3–9
**Dispute:**
Matthew 18:15–35
**Faith:**
Matthew 13:1–9, 18–23
**Friendship:**
Ecclesiastes 4:9–11;
Ephesians 4:29–32
**Grief/Loss:**
2 Samuel 22:2–4;
1 Corinthians 15:51–57;
1 Thessalonians 4:13–18;
Revelation 21:22–22:5
**Loneliness:**
Deuteronomy 31:8;
Matthew 28:20
**Marriage:**
Matthew 19:4–6;
Ephesians 5:25–33
**Money:**
1 Timothy 6:6–10

**Prayer:**
Mark 11:24–26;
Luke 11:1–13
**Repentance and Forgiveness:**
Psalm 32:1–5;
Romans 5:1–8
**Salvation:**
Isaiah 12:1–6;
John 3:13–21;
John 14:1–6;
Romans 1:16–17;
Ephesians 2:4–9;
1 John 4:9–10
**Sick and Infirm:**
Lamentations 3:22–26;
2 Corinthians 4:16–18
**Sin and Temptation:**
Romans 7:18–25;
Ephesians 4:17–24;
1 Corinthians 10:13;
1 John 1:6–9
**Strength:**
Exodus 15:1–11;
Ephesians 6:10–18
**Stress:**
Psalm 131;
Matthew 6:31-34;
Matthew 11:28-30;
Luke 12:13–34;
Philippians 4:5–7
**Wisdom:**
Proverbs 3:5–8
**Witnessing:**
Matthew 5:13–16;
Luke 21:13–15;
Romans 1:16–17

**Work:**
    1 Corinthians 7:17a,
      23–24;
    Colossians 3:23, 24

Then Moses and the people of Israel sang this
    song to the LORD, saying,

"I will sing to the LORD, for He has triumphed
    gloriously;

the horse and his rider He has thrown into
    the sea.

The LORD is my strength and my song,
    and He has become my salvation;

this is my God, and I will praise Him,
    my father's God, and I will exalt Him.

The LORD is a man of war;
    the LORD is His name.

"Pharaoh's chariots and his host He cast
    into the sea,

and his chosen officers were sunk in the
    Red Sea.

The floods covered them;
    they went down into the depths like a stone.

Your right hand, O LORD, glorious in power,
    Your right hand, O LORD, shatters the enemy.

In the greatness of Your majesty You overthrow
    Your adversaries;

You send out Your fury; it consumes them
    like stubble.

At the blast of Your nostrils the waters
    piled up;

the floods stood up in a heap;
 the deeps congealed in the heart of the sea.
The enemy said, 'I will pursue, I will overtake,
 I will divide the spoil, my desire shall have
  its fill of them.
 I will draw my sword; my hand shall
  destroy them.'
You blew with Your wind; the sea covered them;
 they sank like lead in the mighty waters.
"Who is like You, O LORD, among the gods?
Who is like You, majestic in holiness,
awesome in glorious deeds, doing wonders?"

## ↻Early Evening    Exodus 16:11–21, 31

And the LORD said to Moses, "I have heard the grumbling of the people of Israel. Say to them, 'At twilight you shall eat meat, and in the morning you shall be filled with bread. Then you shall know that I am the LORD your God.'"

In the evening quail came up and covered the camp, and in the morning dew lay around the camp. And when the dew had gone up, there was on the face of the wilderness a fine, flake-like thing, fine as frost on the ground. When the people of Israel saw it, they said to one another, "What is it?" For they did not know what it was. And Moses said to them, "It is the bread that the Lord has given you to eat. This is what the Lord has commanded: 'Gather of it, each one of you, as much as he can eat. You shall each take an omer, according to the number of the persons that each of you has in his tent.' " And the people of Israel did so. They gathered, some more, some less. But when they measured it with an omer, whoever gathered much had nothing left over, and whoever gathered little had no lack. Each of them gathered as much as he could eat. And Moses said to them, "Let no one leave any of it over till the morning." But they did not listen to Moses. Some left part of it till the morning, and it bred worms and stank. And Moses was angry with them. Morning by morning they gathered it, each as much as he could eat; but when the sun grew hot, it melted. Now the house of Israel called its name manna. It was like coriander seed, white, and the taste of it was like wafers made with honey.

## ✎Children                    Deuteronomy 6:4–7

Hear, O Israel: The LORD our God, the LORD is one. You shall love the LORD your God with all your heart and with all your soul and with all your might. And these words that I command you today shall be on your heart. You shall teach them diligently to your children, and shall talk of them when you sit in your house, and when you walk by the way, and when you lie down, and when you rise.

### ✏️Loneliness        **Deuteronomy 31:8**

It is the LORD who goes before you. He will be with you; He will not leave you or forsake you. Do not fear or be dismayed.

### ✏️Grief/Loss        **2 Samuel 22:2–4**

The LORD is my rock and my fortress and my
    deliverer,
    my God, my rock, in whom I take refuge,
my shield, and the horn of my salvation,
    my stronghold and my refuge,
    my savior; you save me from violence.
I call upon the LORD, who is worthy to be
    praised,
and I am saved from my enemies.

### ✏️Assurance        **Job 19:21–27**

Have mercy on me, have mercy on me,
    O you my friends,
    for the hand of God has touched me!
Why do you, like God, pursue me?
    Why are you not satisfied with my flesh?
"Oh that my words were written!
    Oh that they were inscribed in a book!
Oh that with an iron pen and lead
    they were engraved in the rock forever!
For I know that my Redeemer lives,
    and at the last He will stand upon the earth.

And after my skin has been thus destroyed,
    yet in my flesh I shall see God,
whom I shall see for myself,
    and my eyes shall behold, and not another.
    My heart faints within me!"

## *Repentance and Forgiveness*    Psalm 32:1–5

Blessed is the one whose transgression is
    forgiven, whose sin is covered.
Blessed is the man against whom the LORD
    counts no iniquity,
    and in whose spirit there is no deceit.
For when I kept silent, my bones wasted away
    through my groaning all day long.
For day and night Your hand was heavy upon me;
    my strength was dried up as by the heat  of
    summer.
I acknowledged my sin to You,
    and I did not cover my iniquity;
I said, "I will confess my transgressions to the
    LORD,"
    and You forgave the iniquity of my sin.

## *Stress*    Psalm 131

O LORD, my heart is not lifted up;
    my eyes are not raised too high;
I do not occupy myself with things

too great and too marvelous for me.
But I have calmed and quieted my soul,
    like a weaned child with its mother;
    like a weaned child is my soul within me.
O Israel, hope in the LORD
    from this time forth and forevermore.

### ✒Assurance                    Psalm 139:1–6

O LORD, You have searched me and known me!
You know when I sit down and when I rise up;
    You discern my thoughts from afar.
You search out my path and my lying down
    And are acquainted with all my ways.
Even before a word is on my tongue,
    behold, O LORD, You know it altogether.
You hem me in, behind and before,
    and lay Your hand upon me.
Such knowledge is too wonderful for me;
    It is high; I cannot attain it.

### ✒Wisdom                    Proverbs 3:5–8

Trust in the LORD with all your heart,
    and do not lean on your own
        understanding.
In all your ways acknowledge Him,
    and He will make straight your paths.
Be not wise in your own eyes;

fear the LORD, and turn away from evil.
It will be healing to your flesh

and refreshment to your bones.

## *Friendship*                    Ecclesiastes 4:9–11

Two are better than one, because they have a
good reward for their toil. For if they fall, one will
lift up his fellow. But woe to him who is alone
when he falls and has not another to lift him up!
Again, if two lie together, they keep warm, but
how can one keep warm alone?

## *Salvation, Morning*              Isaiah 12:1–6

You will say in that day:
"I will give thanks to You, O LORD,

for though You were angry with me,
Your anger turned away,

that You might comfort me.
"Behold, God is my salvation;

I will trust, and will not be afraid;
for the LORD GOD is my strength and my song,

and He has become my salvation."
With joy you will draw water from the wells
of salvation.
And you will say in that day:
"Give thanks to the LORD,

call upon His name,

make known His deeds among the peoples,
    proclaim that His name is exalted.
"Sing praises to the LORD, for He has done
        gloriously;
    let this be made known in all the earth.
Shout, and sing for joy, O inhabitant of Zion,
    for great in your midst is the Holy One of
Israel."

### ✆*Early Evening*                    Isaiah 25:6–9

On this mountain the LORD of hosts will make
for all peoples
a feast of rich food, a feast of well-aged wine,
of rich food full of marrow, of aged wine well
refined.
    And He will swallow up on this mountain
the covering that is cast over all peoples,
the veil that is spread over all nations.
    He will swallow up death forever;
and the LORD GOD will wipe away tears from all
faces,
and the reproach of His people He will take
away from all the earth,
for the LORD has spoken.
    It will be said on that day,
"Behold, this is our God; we have waited for
Him, that He might save us.

This is the LORD; we have waited for Him;
let us be glad and rejoice in His salvation.

### 🕮Assurance                    Isaiah 43:1–3

But now thus says the LORD,
      He who created you, O Jacob,
      He who formed you, O Israel:
"Fear not, for I have redeemed you;
      I have called you by name, you are Mine.
When you pass through the waters, I will be
with you;
      and through the rivers, they shall not over-
whelm you;
when you walk through fire you shall not be
burned,
      and the flame shall not consume you.
For I am the LORD your God,
      the Holy One of Israel, your Savior.

### 🕮Sick                    Lamentations 3:22–26

      The steadfast love of the LORD never ceases;
His mercies never come to an end;
      they are new every morning;
great is Your faithfulness.

      "The LORD is my portion," says my soul,
"therefore I will hope in Him."

      The LORD is good to those who wait for Him,
to the soul who seeks Him.

It is good that one should wait quietly
for the salvation of the LORD.

### ✍Assurance, Close of the Day    Micah 7:18–20

Who is a God like You, pardoning iniquity and passing over transgression for the remnant of His inheritance?

He does not retain His anger forever, because He delights in steadfast love.

He will again have compassion on us; He will tread our iniquities under foot.

You will cast all our sins into the depths of the sea.

You will show faithfulness to Jacob and steadfast love to Abraham,

as You have sworn to our fathers from the days of old.

### ✍Witnessing, Noon         Matthew 5:13–16

[Jesus spoke to them saying,] "You are the salt of the earth, but if salt has lost its taste, how shall its saltiness be restored? It is no longer good for anything except to be thrown out and trampled under people's feet.

"You are the light of the world. A city set on a hill cannot be hidden. Nor do people light a lamp and put it under a basket, but on a stand, and it gives light to all in the house. In the same way, let your light shine before others, so that they may see your good works and give glory to your Father who is in heaven."

### ✒Stress                    Matthew 6:31–34

[Jesus said,] "Therefore do not be anxious, saying, 'What shall we eat?' or 'What shall we drink?' or 'What shall we wear?' For the Gentiles seek after all these things, and your heavenly Father knows that you need them all. But seek first the kingdom of God and His righteousness, and all these things will be added to you.

"Therefore do not be anxious about tomorrow, for tomorrow will be anxious for itself. Sufficient for the day is its own trouble."

### ✒Stress, Close the of Day    Matthew 11:28–30

[Jesus said,] "Come to Me, all who labor and are heavy laden, and I will give you rest. Take My yoke upon you, and learn from Me, for I am gentle and lowly in heart, and you will find rest for your souls. For My yoke is easy, and My burden is light."

### ✒Faith, Noon                Matthew 13:1–9, 18–23

That same day Jesus went out of the house and sat beside the sea. And great crowds gathered about Him, so that He got into a boat and sat down. And the whole crowd stood on the beach.

And He told them many things in parables, saying: "A sower went out to sow. And as he sowed, some seeds fell along the path, and the birds came and devoured them. Other seeds fell on rocky ground, where they did not have much soil, and immediately they sprang up, since they had no depth of soil, but when the sun rose they were scorched. And since they had no root, they withered away. Other seeds fell among thorns, and the thorns grew up and choked them. Other seeds fell on good soil and produced grain, some a hundredfold, some sixty, some thirty. He who has ears, let him hear.

"Hear then the parable of the sower: When anyone hears the word of the kingdom and does not understand it, the evil one comes and snatches away what has been sown in his heart. This is what was sown along the path. As for what was sown on rocky ground, this is the one who hears the word and immediately receives it with joy, yet he has no root in himself, but endures for a while, and when tribulation or persecution arises on account of the word, immediately he falls away. As for what was sown among thorns, this is the one who hears the word, but the cares of the world and the deceitfulness of riches choke the word, and it proves unfruitful. As for what was sown on good soil, this is the one who hears the word and understands it. He indeed bears fruit and yields, in one case a hundredfold, in another sixty, and in another thirty.

### ✎*Early Evening*                    Matthew 14:15–21

Now when it was evening, the disciples came to [Jesus] and said, "This is a desolate place, and the day is now over; send the crowds away to go into the villages and buy food for themselves." But Jesus said, "They need not go away; you give them something to eat." They said to Him, "We have only five loaves here and two fish." And He said, "Bring them here to Me." Then He ordered the crowds to sit down on the grass, and taking the five loaves and the two fish, He looked up to heaven and said a blessing. Then He broke the loaves and gave them to the disciples, and the disciples gave them to the crowds. And they all ate and were satisfied. And they took up twelve baskets full of the broken pieces left over. And those who ate were about five thousand men, besides women and children.

### ✎*Children*                        Matthew 18:2–6

And calling to Him a child, [Jesus] put him in the midst of them and said, "Truly, I say to you, unless you turn and become like children, you will never enter the kingdom of heaven. Whoever humbles himself like this child is the greatest in the kingdom of heaven.

"Whoever receives one such child in My name receives Me, but whoever causes one of these little ones who believe in Me to sin, it would be better for him to have a great millstone fastened around his neck and to be drowned in the depth of the sea."

## ◯Dispute, Close of the Day
### Matthew 18:15–35

[Jesus said to them] "If your brother sins against you, go and tell him his fault, between you and him alone. If he listens to you, you have gained your brother. But if he does not listen, take one or two others along with you, that every charge may be established by the evidence of two or three witnesses. If he refuses to listen to them, tell it to the church. And if he refuses to listen even to the church, let him be to you as a Gentile and a tax collector. Truly, I say to you, whatever you bind on earth shall be bound in heaven, and whatever you loose on earth shall be loosed in heaven. Again I say to you, if two of you agree on earth about anything they ask, it will be done for them by My Father in heaven. For where two or three are gathered in My name, there am I among them."

Then Peter came up and said to Him, "Lord, how often will my brother sin against me, and I forgive him? As many as seven times?" Jesus said to him, "I do not say to you seven times, but seventy times seven.

"Therefore the kingdom of heaven may be compared to a king who wished to settle accounts with his servants. When he began to settle, one was brought to him who owed him ten thousand talents. And since he could not pay, his master ordered him to be sold, with his wife and children and all that he had, and payment to be made. So the servant fell on his knees, imploring him, 'Have patience with me, and I will pay you everything.' And out of pity for him, the master of that servant released him and forgave him the debt. But when that same servant went out, he found one of his fellow servants who owed him a hundred denarii, and seizing him, he began to choke him, saying, 'Pay what you owe.' So his fellow servant fell down and pleaded with him, 'Have patience with me, and I will pay you.' He refused and went and put him in prison until he should pay the debt. When his fellow servants saw what had taken place, they were greatly distressed, and they went and reported to their master all that had taken place. Then his master summoned him and said to him, 'You wicked servant! I forgave you all that debt because you pleaded with me. And should not you have had mercy on your fellow servant, as I had mercy on you?' And in anger his master delivered him to the jailers, until he should pay all his debt. So also My heavenly Father will do to every one of you, if you do not forgive your brother from your heart."

### ⌀Marriage                              Matthew 19:4–6

[Jesus] answered, "Have you not read that He who created them from the beginning made them male and female, and said, 'Therefore a man shall leave his father and his mother and hold fast to his wife, and they shall become one flesh'? So they are no longer two but one flesh. What therefore God has joined together, let not man separate."

### ⌀Morning                              Matthew 20:1–16

[Jesus told them this parable,] "For the kingdom of heaven is like a master of a house who went out early in the morning to hire laborers for his vineyard. After agreeing with the laborers for a denarius a day, he sent them into his vineyard. And going out about the third hour he saw others standing idle in the marketplace, and to them he said, 'You go into the vineyard too, and whatever is right I will give you.' So they went. Going out again about the sixth hour and the ninth hour, he did the same. And about the eleventh hour he went out and found others standing. And he said to them, 'Why do you stand here idle all day?' They said to him, 'Because no one has hired us.' He said to them, 'You go into the vineyard too.' And when evening came, the owner of the vineyard said to his foreman, 'Call the laborers and pay them their wages, beginning with the last, up to the first.' And when those hired about the eleventh hour came, each of them received a denarius. Now when those hired first came, they thought they would receive more, but each of them also received a denarius. And on receiving it they grumbled at the master of the house, saying, 'These last worked only one hour, and you have made them equal to us who have borne the burden of the day and the scorching heat.' But he replied to one of them, 'Friend, I am doing you no wrong. Did you not agree with me for a denarius? Take what belongs to you and go. I choose to give to this last worker as I give to you. Am I not allowed to do what I choose with what belongs to me? Or do you begrudge my generosity?' So the last will be first, and the first last."

## ✑Christian Life, Close of the Day
### Matthew 25:1–13

[Jesus told them this parable,]"Then the kingdom of heaven will be like ten virgins who took their lamps and went to meet the bridegroom. Five of them were foolish, and five were wise. For when the foolish took their lamps, they took no oil with them, but the wise took flasks of oil with their lamps. As the bridegroom was delayed, they all became drowsy and slept. But at midnight there was a cry, 'Here is the bridegroom! Come out to meet him.' Then all those virgins rose and trimmed their lamps. And the foolish said to the wise, 'Give us some of your oil, for our lamps are going out.' But the wise answered, saying, 'Since there will not be enough for us and for you, go rather to the dealers and buy for yourselves.' And while they were going to buy, the bridegroom came, and those who were ready went in with him to the marriage feast, and the door was shut. Afterward the other virgins came also, saying, 'Lord, lord, open to us.' But he answered, 'Truly, I say to you, I do not know you.' Watch therefore, for you know neither the day nor the hour."

### ✑*Early Evening*        Matthew 27:57–60

When it was evening, there came a rich man from Arimathea, named Joseph, who also was a disciple of Jesus. He went to Pilate and asked for the body of Jesus. Then Pilate ordered it to be given to him. And Joseph took the body and wrapped it in a clean linen shroud and laid it in his own new tomb, which he had cut in the rock. And he rolled a great stone to the entrance of the tomb and went away.

### ✑*Loneliness*        Matthew 28:20b

[Jesus said,] "Behold, I am with you always, to the end of the age."

### ✑*Prayer*        Mark 11:24–26

[Jesus spoke to them saying,] "Therefore I tell you, whatever you ask in prayer, believe that you have received it, and it will be yours. And whenever you stand praying, forgive, if you have anything against anyone, so that your Father also who is in heaven may forgive you your trespasses. But if you do not forgive, neither will your Father who is in heaven forgive your trespasses."

## ✎Noon                                    Mark 13:23–27

[Jesus spoke to them saying,] "But be on guard; I have told you all things beforehand. But in those days, after that tribulation, the sun will be darkened, and the moon will not give its light, and the stars will be falling from heaven, and the powers in the heavens will be shaken. And then they will see the Son of Man coming in clouds with great power and glory. And then He will send out the angels and gather His elect from the four winds, from the ends of the earth to the ends of heaven."

## ✎Morning                                 Mark 13:32–37

[Jesus spoke to them saying,] "But concerning that day or that hour, no one knows, not even the angels in heaven, nor the Son, but only the Father. Be on guard, keep awake. For you do not know when the time will come. It is like a man going on a journey, when he leaves home and puts his servants in charge, each with his work, and commands the doorkeeper to stay awake. Therefore stay awake—for you do not know when the master of the house will come, in the evening, or at midnight, or when the cock crows, or in the morning—lest he come suddenly and find you asleep. And what I say to you I say to all: Stay awake."

## ⌘The Birth of Jesus                    Luke 2:1–20

In those days a decree went out from Caesar Augustus that all the world should be registered. This was the first registration when Quirinius was governor of Syria. And all went to be registered, each to his own town. And Joseph also went up from Galilee, from the town of Nazareth, to Judea, to the city of David, which is called Bethlehem, because he was of the house and lineage of David, to be registered with Mary, his betrothed, who was with child. And while they were there, the time came for her to give birth. And she gave birth to her firstborn son and wrapped him in swaddling cloths and laid him in a manger, because there was no place for them in the inn.

And in the same region there were shepherds out in the field, keeping watch over their flock by night. And an angel of the Lord appeared to them, and the glory of the Lord shone around them, and they were filled with fear. And the angel said to them, "Fear not, for behold, I bring you good news of a great joy that will be for all the people. For unto you is born this day in the city of David a Savior, who is Christ the Lord. And this will be a sign for you: you will find a baby wrapped in swaddling cloths and lying in a manger." And suddenly there was with the angel a multitude of the heavenly host praising God and saying,

"Glory to God in the highest, and on earth peace among those with whom He is pleased!"

When the angels went away from them into heaven, the shepherds said to one another, "Let us go over to Bethlehem and see this thing that has happened, which the Lord has made known to us." And they went with haste and found Mary and Joseph, and the baby lying in a manger. And when they saw it, they made known the saying that had been told them concerning this child. And all who heard it wondered at what the shepherds told them. But Mary treasured up all these things, pondering them in her heart. And the shepherds returned, glorifying and praising God for all they had heard and seen, as it had been told them.

### ✋Prayer, Close of the Day        Luke 11:1–13

Now Jesus was praying in a certain place, and when He finished, one of His disciples said to Him, "Lord, teach us to pray, as John taught his disciples." And He said to them,

"When you pray, say:
"Father, hallowed be Your name.
Your kingdom come.

Give us each day our daily bread,
and forgive us our sins,
as we forgive everyone who [sins against] us.
And lead us not into temptation."

And He said to them, "Which of you who has a friend will go to him at midnight and say to him, 'Friend, lend me three loaves, for a friend of mine has arrived on a journey, and I have nothing to set before him'; and he will answer from within, 'Do not bother me; the door is now shut, and my children are with me in bed. I cannot get up and give you anything'? I tell you, though he will not get up and give him anything because he is his friend, yet because of his impudence he will rise and give him whatever he needs. And I tell you, ask, and it will be given to you; seek, and you will find; knock, and it will be opened to you. For everyone who asks receives, and the one who seeks finds, and to the one who knocks it will be opened. What father among you, if his son asks for a fish, will instead of a fish give him a serpent; or if he asks for an egg, will give him a scorpion? If you then, who are evil, know how to give good gifts to your children, how much more will the heavenly Father give the Holy Spirit to those who ask Him!"

## ⏾Stress, Close of the Day      Luke 12:13–34

Someone in the crowd said to [Jesus], "Teacher,

tell my brother to divide the inheritance with me." But He said to him, "Man, who made me a judge or arbitrator over you?" And He said to them, "Take care, and be on your guard against all covetousness, for one's life does not consist in the abundance of his possessions." And He told them a parable, saying, "The land of a rich man produced plentifully, and he thought to himself, 'What shall I do, for I have nowhere to store my crops?' And he said, 'I will do this: I will tear down my barns and build larger ones, and there I will store all my grain and my goods. And I will say to my soul, Soul, you have ample goods laid up for many years; relax, eat, drink, be merry.' But God said to him, 'Fool! This night your soul is required of you, and the things you have prepared, whose will they be?' So is the one who lays up treasure for himself and is not rich toward God."

And He said to His disciples, "Therefore I tell you, do not be anxious about your life, what you will eat, nor about your body, what you will put on. For life is more than food, and the body more than clothing. Consider the ravens: they neither sow nor reap, they have neither storehouse nor barn, and yet God feeds them. Of how much more value are you than the birds! And which of you by being anxious can add a single hour to his span of life? If then you are not able to do as small a thing as that, why are you anxious about the rest? Consider the lilies, how they grow: they neither toil nor spin, yet I tell you, even Solomon in all his glory was not arrayed like one of these. But if God so clothes the grass, which is alive in the field today, and tomorrow is thrown into the oven, how much more will He clothe you, O you of little faith! And do not seek what you are to eat and what you are to drink, nor be worried. For all the nations of the world seek after these things, and your Father knows that you need them. Instead, seek His kingdom, and these things will be added to you.

"Fear not, little flock, for it is your Father's good pleasure to give you the kingdom. Sell your possessions, and give to the needy. Provide yourselves with moneybags that do not grow old, with a treasure in the heavens that does not fail, where no thief approaches and no moth destroys. For where your treasure is, there will your heart be also."

### ✿Evening Prayer                    Luke 14:15–24

When one of those who reclined at table with [Jesus] heard these things, He said to him, "Blessed is everyone who will eat bread in the kingdom of God!" But [Jesus] said to him, "A man once gave a great banquet and invited many. And at the time for the banquet he sent his servant to say to those who had been invited, 'Come, for everything is now ready.' But they all alike began to make excuses. The first said to him, 'I have bought a field, and I must go out and see it. Please have me excused.' And another said, 'I have bought five yoke of oxen, and I go to examine them. Please have me excused.' And another said, 'I have married a wife, and therefore I cannot come.' So the servant came and reported these things to his master. Then the master of the house became angry and said to his servant, 'Go out quickly to the streets and lanes of the city, and bring in the poor and crippled and blind and lame.' And the servant said, 'Sir, what you commanded has been done, and still there is room.' And the master said to the servant, 'Go out to the highways and hedges and compel people to come in, that my house may be filled. For I tell you, none of those men who were invited shall taste my banquet.' "

### 🖎 Witnessing                                    Luke 21:13–15

[Jesus said to them,] "This will be your opportunity to bear witness. Settle it therefore in your minds not to meditate beforehand how to answer, for I will give you a mouth and wisdom, which none of your adversaries will be able to withstand or contradict."

### 🖎 Noon Prayer                                    Luke 23:44–46

It was now about the sixth hour, and there was darkness over the whole land until the ninth hour, while the sun's light failed. And the curtain of the temple was torn in two. Then Jesus, calling out with a loud voice, said, "Father, into Your hands I commit My spirit!" And having said this He breathed his last.

### ꙩMorning, The Resurrection of Jesus

Luke 24:1–8

But on the first day of the week, at early dawn, they went to [Jesus'] tomb, taking the spices they had prepared. And they found the stone rolled away from the tomb, but when they went in they did not find the body of the Lord Jesus. While they were perplexed about this, behold, two men stood by them in dazzling apparel. And as they were frightened and bowed their faces to the ground, the men said to them, "Why do you seek the living among the dead? He is not here, but has risen. Remember how He told you, while He was still in Galilee, that the Son of Man must be delivered into the hands of sinful men and be crucified and on the third day rise." And they remembered His words.

### ꙩ Early Evening                    Luke 24:28–31

So they drew near to the village to which they were going. [The Lord] acted as if He were going farther, but they urged Him strongly, saying, "Stay with us, for it is toward evening and the day is now far spent." So He went in to stay with them. When He was at table with them, He took the bread and blessed and broke it and gave it to them. And their eyes were opened, and they recognized Him. And He vanished from their sight.

### ◯Salvation                              John 3:13–21

[Jesus spoke to them saying,] "No one has ascended into heaven except He who descended from heaven, the Son of Man. And as Moses lifted up the serpent in the wilderness, so must the Son of Man be lifted up, that whoever believes in Him may have eternal life. For God so loved the world, that He gave His only Son, that whoever believes in Him should not perish but have eternal life. For God did not send His Son into the world to condemn the world, but in order that the world might be saved through Him. Whoever believes in Him is not condemned, but whoever does not believe is condemned already, because he has not believed in the name of the only Son of God. And this is the judgment: the light has come into the world, and people loved the darkness rather than the light because their deeds were evil. For everyone who does wicked things hates the light and does not come to the light, lest his deeds should be exposed. But whoever does what is true comes to the light, so that it may be clearly seen that his deeds have been carried out in God."

When they found Him on the other side of the sea, they said to Him, "Rabbi, when did You come here?" Jesus answered them, "Truly, truly, I say to you, you are seeking Me, not because you saw signs, but because you ate your fill of the loaves. Do not labor for the food that perishes, but for the food that endures to eternal life, which the Son of Man will give to you. For on Him God the Father has set His seal." Then they said to Him, "What must we do, to be doing the works of God?" Jesus answered them, "This is the work of God, that you believe in Him whom He has sent." So they said to Him, "Then what sign do you do, that we may see and believe You? What work do You perform? Our fathers ate the manna in the wilderness; as it is written, 'He gave them bread from heaven to eat.'" Jesus then said to them, "Truly, truly, I say to you, it was not Moses who gave you the bread from heaven, but My Father gives you the true bread from heaven. For the bread of God is He who comes down from heaven and gives life to the world." They said to Him, "Sir, give us this bread always."

Jesus said to them, "I am the bread of life; whoever comes to Me shall not hunger, and whoever believes in Me shall never thirst."

So Jesus again said to them, "Truly, truly, I say to you, I am the door of the sheep. All who came before Me are thieves and robbers, but the sheep did not listen to them. I am the door. If anyone enters by Me, he will be saved and will go in and out and find pasture. The thief comes only to steal and kill and destroy. I came that they may have life and have it abundantly. I am the good shepherd. The good shepherd lays down his life for the sheep. He who is a hired hand and not a shepherd, who does not own the sheep, sees the wolf coming and leaves the sheep and flees, and the wolf snatches them and scatters them. He flees because he is a hired hand and cares nothing for the sheep. I am the good shepherd. I know My own and My own know Me, just as the Father knows Me and I know the Father; and I lay down My life for the sheep. And I have other sheep that are not of this fold. I must bring them also, and they will listen to My voice. So there will be one flock, one shepherd. For this reason the Father loves Me, because I lay down My life that I may take it up again. No one takes it from Me, but I lay it down of My own accord. I have authority to lay it down, and I have authority to take it up again. This charge I have received from My Father."

## ⊘Salvation                          John 14:1–6

"Let not your hearts be troubled [said Jesus].
Believe in God; believe also in Me. In My Father's
house are many rooms. If it were not so, would I
have told you that I go to prepare a place for you?
And if I go and prepare a place for you, I will
come again and will take you to Myself, that
where I am you may be also. And you know the
way to where I am going." Thomas said to Him,
"Lord, we do not know where You are going. How
can we know the way?" Jesus said to him, "I am
the way, and the truth, and the life. No one comes
to the Father except through Me."

## ⊘Noon                             John 15:1–9

[Jesus spoke to them saying,] "I am the true vine,
and My Father is the vinedresser. Every branch of
Mine that does not bear fruit He takes away, and
every branch that does bear fruit He prunes, that
it may bear more fruit. Already you are clean
because of the word that I have spoken to you.
Abide in Me, and I in you. As the branch cannot
bear fruit by itself, unless it abides in the vine,
neither can you, unless you abide in Me. I am the
vine; you are the branches. Whoever abides in
Me and I in him, he it is that bears much fruit, for
apart from Me you can do nothing. If anyone
does not abide in Me he is thrown away like a
branch and withers; and the branches are gath-

ered, thrown into the fire, and burned. If you abide in Me, and My words abide in you, ask whatever you wish, and it will be done for you. By this My Father is glorified, that you bear much fruit and so prove to be My disciples. As the Father has loved Me, so have I loved you. Abide in My love."

## ✆The Death and Burial of Jesus

### John 19:16–42

So [Pilate] delivered [Jesus] over to them to be crucified.

So they took Jesus, and He went out, bearing His own cross, to the place called the place of a skull, which in Aramaic is called Golgotha.

There they crucified Him, and with Him two others, one on either side, and Jesus between them. Pilate also wrote an inscription and put it on the cross. It read, "Jesus of Nazareth, the King of the Jews." Many of the Jews read this inscription, for the place where Jesus was crucified was near the city, and it was written in Aramaic, in Latin, and in Greek. So the chief priests of the Jews said to Pilate, "Do not write, 'The King of the Jews,' but rather, 'This man said, I am King of the Jews.' " Pilate answered, "What I have written I have written."

When the soldiers had crucified Jesus, they took His garments and divided them into four parts, one part for each soldier; also His tunic. But the tunic was seamless, woven in one piece from top to bottom, so they said to one another, "Let us not tear it, but cast lots for it to see whose it shall be." This was to fulfill the Scripture which says,

"They divided My garments among them, and for My clothing they cast lots."

So the soldiers did these things, but standing by the cross of Jesus were His mother and His mother's sister, Mary the wife of Clopas, and Mary Magdalene. When Jesus saw His mother and the disciple whom He loved standing nearby, He said to His mother, "Woman, behold, your son!" Then He said to the disciple, "Behold, your mother!" And from that hour the disciple took her to his own home.

After this, Jesus, knowing that all was now finished, said (to fulfill the Scripture), "I thirst." A jar full of sour wine stood there, so they put a sponge full of the sour wine on a hyssop branch and held it to His mouth. When Jesus had received the sour wine, He said, "It is finished," and He bowed His head and gave up His spirit.

Since it was the day of Preparation, and so that the bodies would not remain on the cross on the Sabbath (for that Sabbath was a high day), the Jews asked Pilate that their legs might be broken and that they might be taken away. So the soldiers came and broke the legs of the first, and of the other who had been crucified with Him. But when they came to Jesus and saw that He was already dead, they did not break His legs. But one of the soldiers pierced His side with a spear, and at once there came out blood and water. He who saw it has borne witness—his testimony is true, and he knows that he is telling the truth—that you also may believe. For these things took place that the Scripture might be fulfilled: "Not one of His bones will be broken." And again another Scripture says, "They will look on Him whom they have pierced."

After these things Joseph of Arimathea, who was a disciple of Jesus, but secretly for fear of the Jews, asked Pilate that he might take away the body of Jesus, and Pilate gave him permission. So he came and took away His body. Nicodemus also, who earlier had come to Jesus by night, came bringing a mixture of myrrh and aloes, about seventy-five pounds in weight. So they took the body of Jesus and bound it in linen cloths with the spices, as is the burial custom of the Jews. Now in the place where He was crucified there was a garden, and in the garden a new tomb in which no one had yet been laid. So because of the Jewish day of Preparation, since the tomb was close at hand, they laid Jesus there.

### ✎Morning                    John 21:4–14

Just as day was breaking, Jesus stood on the

shore; yet the disciples did not know that it was Jesus. Jesus said to them, "Children, do you have any fish?" They answered Him, "No." He said to them, "Cast the net on the right side of the boat, and you will find some." So they cast it, and now they were not able to haul it in, because of the quantity of fish. That disciple whom Jesus loved therefore said to Peter, "It is the Lord!" When Simon Peter heard that it was the Lord, he put on his outer garment, for he was stripped for work, and threw himself into the sea. The other disciples came in the boat, dragging the net full of fish, for they were not far from the land, but about a hundred yards off.

When they got out on land, they saw a charcoal fire in place, with fish laid out on it, and bread. Jesus said to them, "Bring some of the fish that you have just caught." So Simon Peter went aboard and hauled the net ashore, full of large fish, 153 of them. And although there were so many, the net was not torn. Jesus said to them, "Come and have breakfast." Now none of the disciples dared ask Him, "Who are You?" They knew it was the Lord. Jesus came and took the bread and gave it to them, and so with the fish. This was now the third time that Jesus was revealed to the disciples after He was raised from the dead.

### ✎Witnessing, Salvation          Romans 1:16–17

For I am not ashamed of the gospel, for it is the

power of God for salvation to everyone who believes, to the Jew first and also to the Greek. For in it the righteousness of God is revealed from faith for faith, as it is written, "The righteous shall live by faith."

### ✒Repentance and Forgiveness    Romans 5:1–8

Therefore, since we have been justified by faith, we have peace with God through our Lord Jesus Christ. Through Him we have also obtained access by faith into this grace in which we stand, and we rejoice in hope of the glory of God. More than that, we rejoice in our sufferings, knowing that suffering produces endurance, and endurance produces character, and character produces hope, and hope does not put us to shame, because God's love has been poured into our hearts through the Holy Spirit who has been given to us.

For while we were still weak, at the right time Christ died for the ungodly. For one will scarcely die for a righteous person—though perhaps for a good person one would dare even to die—but God shows His love for us in that while we were still sinners, Christ died for us.

### ✒Christian Life, Morning    Romans 6:1–4

What shall we say then? Are we to continue in sin that grace may abound? By no means! How can we who died to sin still live in it? Do you not know that all of us who have been baptized into Christ Jesus were baptized into His death? We were buried therefore with Him by baptism into death, in order that, just as Christ was raised from the dead by the glory of the Father, we too might walk in newness of life.

## ✒Sin and Temptation, Noon   Romans 7:18–25

For I know that nothing good dwells in me, that is, in my flesh. For I have the desire to do what is right, but not the ability to carry it out. For I do not do the good I want, but the evil I do not want is what I keep on doing. Now if I do what I do not want, it is no longer I who do it, but sin that dwells within me.

So I find it to be a law that when I want to do right, evil lies close at hand. For I delight in the law of God, in my inner being, but I see in my members another law waging war against the law of my mind and making me captive to the law of sin that dwells in my members. Wretched man that I am! Who will deliver me from this body of death? Thanks be to God through Jesus Christ our Lord! So then, I myself serve the law of God with my mind, but with my flesh I serve the law of sin.

## ✒Assurance; Close of Day        Romans 8:31–39

What then shall we say to these things? If God is for us, who can be against us? He who did not spare His own Son but gave Him up for us all, how will He not also with Him graciously give us all things? Who shall bring any charge against God's elect? It is God who justifies. Who is to condemn? Christ Jesus is the one who died—more than that, who was raised—who is at the right hand of God, who indeed is interceding for us. Who shall separate us from the love of Christ? Shall tribulation, or distress, or persecution, or famine, or nakedness, or danger, or sword? As it is written,

"For your sake we are being killed all the day long; we are regarded as sheep to be slaughtered."

No, in all these things we are more than conquerors through Him who loved us. For I am sure that neither death nor life, nor angels nor rulers, nor things present nor things to come, nor powers, nor height nor depth, nor anything else in all creation, will be able to separate us from the love of God in Christ Jesus our Lord.

## ✆Noon                                          Romans 12:1–2

I appeal to you therefore, brothers, by the mercies of God, to present your bodies as a living sacrifice, holy and acceptable to God, which is your spiritual worship. Do not be conformed to this world, but be transformed by the renewal of your mind, that by testing you may discern what is the will of God, what is good and acceptable and perfect.

### ✎*Work, Noon*  1 Corinthians 7:17a, 23–24

Only let each person lead the life that the Lord has assigned to him, and to which God has called him. You were bought with a price; do not become slaves of men. So, brothers, in whatever condition each was called, there let him remain with God.

### ✎*Sin and Temptation*  1 Corinthians 10:13

No temptation has overtaken you that is not common to man. God is faithful, and He will not let you be tempted beyond your ability, but with the temptation He will also provide the way of escape, that you may be able to endure it.

### *Grief/Loss*  1 Corinthians 15:51–57

Behold! I tell you a mystery. We shall not all sleep, but we shall all be changed, in a moment, in the twinkling of an eye, at the last trumpet. For the trumpet will sound, and the dead will be raised imperishable, and we shall be changed. For this perishable body must put on the imperishable, and this mortal body must put on immortality. When the perishable puts on the imperishable, and the mortal puts on immortality, then shall come to pass the saying that is written:

"Death is swallowed up in victory."

"O death, where is your victory?

O death, where is your sting?"

The sting of death is sin, and the power of sin is the law. But thanks be to God, who gives us the victory through our Lord Jesus Christ.

### ✑Sick and Infirm, Close of Day
#### 2 Corinthians 4:16–18

So we do not lose heart. Though our outer nature is wasting away, our inner nature is being renewed day by day. For this slight momentary affliction is preparing for us an eternal weight of glory beyond all comparison, as we look not to the things that are seen but to the things that are unseen. For the things that are seen are transient, but the things that are unseen are eternal.

### ✑Salvation                    Ephesians 2:4–9

But God, being rich in mercy, because of the great love with which he loved us, even when we were dead in our trespasses, made us alive together with Christ—by grace you have been saved—and raised us up with him and seated us with him in the heavenly places in Christ Jesus, so that in the coming ages he might show the immeasurable riches of his grace in kindness toward us in Christ Jesus. For by grace you have been saved through faith. And this is not your own doing; it is the gift of God, not a result of works, so that no one may boast.

## ᴑSin and Temptation, Morning Prayer
### Ephesians 4:17–24

Now this I say and testify in the Lord, that you must no longer walk as the Gentiles do, in the futility of their minds. They are darkened in their understanding, alienated from the life of God because of the ignorance that is in them, due to their hardness of heart. They have become callous and have given themselves up to sensuality, greedy to practice every kind of impurity. But that is not the way you learned Christ!—assuming that you have heard about Him and were taught in Him, as the truth is in Jesus, to put off your old self, which belongs to your former manner of life and is corrupt through deceitful desires, and to be renewed in the spirit of your minds, and to put on the new self, created after the likeness of God in true righteousness and holiness.

## ᴑFriendship
### Ephesians 4:29–32

Let no corrupting talk come out of your mouths, but only such as is good for building up, as fits the occasion, that it may give grace to those who hear. And do not grieve the Holy Spirit of God, by whom you were sealed for the day of redemption. Let all bitterness and wrath and anger and clamor and slander be put away from you, along with all malice. Be kind to one another, tenderhearted, forgiving one another, as God in Christ forgave you.

Therefore be imitators of God, as beloved children. And walk in love, as Christ loved us and gave Himself up for us, a fragrant offering and sacrifice to God.

But sexual immorality and all impurity or covetousness must not even be named among you, as is proper among saints. Let there be no filthiness nor foolish talk nor crude joking, which are out of place, but instead let there be thanksgiving.

❧*Marriage*                          Ephesians 5:25–33

Husbands, love your wives, as Christ loved the church and gave Himself up for her, that He might sanctify her, having cleansed her by the washing of water with the word, so that He might present the church to Himself in splendor, without spot or wrinkle or any such thing, that she might be holy and without blemish. In the same way husbands should love their wives as their own bodies. He who loves his wife loves himself. For no one ever hated his own flesh, but nourishes and cherishes it, just as Christ does the church, because we are members of His body. "Therefore a man shall leave his father and mother and hold fast to his wife, and the two shall become one flesh." This mystery is profound, and I am saying that it refers to Christ and the church.

However, let each one of you love his wife as him-self, and let the wife see that she respects her hus-band.

### ✆Children                                    Ephesians 6:4

Fathers, do not provoke your children to anger, but bring them up in the discipline and instruc-tion of the Lord.

### ✆Strength, Early Evening
Ephesians 6:10–18

Finally, be strong in the Lord and in the strength of His might. Put on the whole armor of God, that you may be able to stand against the schemes of the devil. For we do not wrestle against flesh and blood, but against the rulers, against the author-ities, against the cosmic powers over this present darkness, against the spiritual forces of evil in the heavenly places. Therefore take up the whole armor of God, that you may be able to withstand in the evil day, and having done all, to stand firm. Stand therefore, having fastened on the belt of truth, and having put on the breastplate of righteousness, and, as shoes for your feet, having put on the readiness given by the gospel of peace. In all circumstances take up the shield of faith, with which you can extinguish all the flaming darts of the evil one; and take the helmet of sal-vation, and the sword of the Spirit, which is the word of God, praying at all times in the Spirit,

with all prayer and supplication. To that end
keep alert with all perseverance, making supplication for all the saints.

### ✐Stress                            Philippians 4:5–7

Let your reasonableness be known to everyone.
The Lord is at hand; do not be anxious about
anything, but in everything by prayer and supplication with thanksgiving let your requests be
made known to God. And the peace of God,
which surpasses all understanding, will guard
your hearts and your minds in Christ Jesus.

### ✐Assurance, Morning          Colossians 3:1–4

If then you have been raised with Christ, seek the
things that are above, where Christ is, seated at
the right hand of God. Set your minds on things
that are above, not on things that are on earth.
For you have died, and your life is hidden with
Christ in God. When Christ who is your life
appears, then you also will appear with Him in
glory.

### ✐Work                            Colossians 3:23, 24

Whatever you do, work heartily, as for the Lord
and not for men, knowing that from the Lord you
will receive the inheritance as your reward. You
are serving the Lord Christ.

## ☙Grief/Loss                    1 Thessalonians 4:13–18

But we do not want you to be uninformed, brothers, about those who are asleep, that you may not grieve as others do who have no hope. For since we believe that Jesus died and rose again, even so, through Jesus, God will bring with Him those who have fallen asleep. For this we declare to you by a word from the Lord, that we who are alive, who are left until the coming of the Lord, will not precede those who have fallen asleep. For the Lord Himself will descend from heaven with a cry of command, with the voice of an archangel, and with the sound of the trumpet of God. And the dead in Christ will rise first. Then we who are alive, who are left, will be caught up together with them in the clouds to meet the Lord in the air, and so we will always be with the Lord. Therefore encourage one another with these words.

## ☙Money                          1 Timothy 6:6–10

Now there is great gain in godliness with contentment, for we brought nothing into the world, and we cannot take anything out of the world. But if we have food and clothing, with these we will be content. But those who desire to be rich fall into temptation, into a snare, into many senseless and harmful desires that plunge people into ruin and destruction. For the love of money is a root of all kinds of evils. It is through this craving that some have wandered away from the faith and pierced themselves with many pangs.

## ✑Confidence          Hebrews 10:35–36

Therefore do not throw away your confidence, which has a great reward. For you have need of endurance, so that when you have done the will of God you may receive what is promised.

## ✑Confidence          Hebrews 12:1–11

Therefore, since we are surrounded by so great a cloud of witnesses, let us also lay aside every weight, and sin which clings so closely, and let us run with endurance the race that is set before us, looking to Jesus, the founder and perfecter of our faith, who for the joy that was set before him endured the cross, despising the shame, and is seated at the right hand of the throne of God.

Consider him who endured from sinners such hostility against himself, so that you may not grow weary or fainthearted. In your struggle against sin you have not yet resisted to the point of shedding your blood. And have you forgotten the exhortation that addresses you as sons? "My son, do not regard lightly the discipline of the Lord,nor be weary when reproved by him. For the Lord disciplines the one he loves, and chastises every son whom he receives."

It is for discipline that you have to endure. God is

treating you as sons. For what son is there whom his father does not discipline? If you are left without discipline, in which all have participated, then you are illegitimate children and not sons. Besides this, we have had earthly fathers who disciplined us and we respected them. Shall we not much more be subject to the Father of spirits and live? For they disciplined us for a short time as it seemed best to them, but he disciplines us for our good, that we may share his holiness. For the moment all discipline seems painful rather than pleasant, but later it yields the peaceful fruit of righteousness to those who have been trained by it.

### ✐*Confidence, Noon*                    1 Peter 1:3–9

Blessed be the God and Father of our Lord Jesus Christ! According to His great mercy, He has caused us to be born again to a living hope through the resurrection of Jesus Christ from the dead, to an inheritance that is imperishable, undefiled, and unfading, kept in heaven for you, who by God's power are being guarded through faith for a salvation ready to be revealed in the last time. In this you rejoice, though now for a little while, if necessary, you have been grieved by various trials, so that the tested genuineness of your faith—more precious than gold that perishes though it is tested by fire—may be found to result in praise and glory and honor at the revelation of Jesus Christ. Though you have not seen Him, you love Him. Though you do not now see Him, you believe in Him and rejoice with joy that is inexpressible and filled with glory, obtaining the outcome of your faith, the salvation of your souls.

## *Sin and Temptation*                    1 John 1:6–9

If we say we have fellowship with Him while we walk in darkness, we lie and do not practice the truth. But if we walk in the light, as He is in the light, we have fellowship with one another, and the blood of Jesus His Son cleanses us from all sin. If we say we have no sin, we deceive ourselves, and the truth is not in us. If we confess our sins, He is faithful and just to forgive us our sins and to cleanse us from all unrighteousness.

## *Assurance*                             1 John 3:1–2

See what kind of love the Father has given to us, that we should be called children of God; and so we are. The reason why the world does not know us is that it did not know Him. Beloved, we are God's children now, and what we will be has not yet appeared; but we know that when He appears we shall be like Him, because we shall see Him as He is.

## *Salvation*                            1 John 4:7–10

Beloved, let us love one another, for love is from God, and whoever loves has been born of God and knows God. Anyone who does not love does not know God, because God is love. In this the love of God was made manifest among us, that God sent His only Son into the world, so that we might live through Him. In this is love, not that we have loved God but that He loved us and sent His Son to be the propitiation for our sins.

### ✍Christian Life                    Jude 20–25

But you, beloved, build yourselves up in your most holy faith; pray in the Holy Spirit; keep yourselves in the love of God, waiting for the mercy of our Lord Jesus Christ that leads to eternal life. And have mercy on those who doubt; save others by snatching them out of the fire; to others show mercy with fear, hating even the garment stained by the flesh.

Now to Him who is able to keep you from stumbling and to present you blameless before the presence of his glory with great joy, to the only God, our Savior, through Jesus Christ our Lord, be glory, majesty, dominion, and authority, before all time and now and forever. Amen.

### ✍Grief/Loss, Close of the Day
### Revelation 21:22–22:5

And I saw no temple in the city, for its temple is the Lord God the Almighty and the Lamb. And the city has no need of sun or moon to shine on it, for the glory of God gives it light, and its lamp is the Lamb. By its light will the nations walk, and the kings of the earth will bring their glory into it, and its gates will never be shut by day—and there will be no night there. They will bring into it the glory and the honor of the nations. But nothing unclean will ever enter it, nor anyone who does what is detestable or false, but only those who are written in the Lamb's book of life.

Then the angel showed me the river of the water of life, bright as crystal, flowing from the throne of God and of the Lamb through the middle of the street of the city; also, on either side of the river, the tree of life with its twelve kinds of fruit, yielding its fruit each month. The leaves of the tree were for the healing of the nations. No longer will there be anything accursed, but the throne of God and of the Lamb will be in it, and His servants will worship Him. They will see His face, and His name will be on their foreheads. And night will be no more. They will need no light of lamp or sun, for the Lord God will be their light, and they will reign forever and ever.

# PRAYERS FOR OURSELVES
# AND OTHERS

# 1.

## The Church Year

### ❧ *Advent*

O Lord Jesus Christ, our King and Redeemer, to who Your faithful people have ever cried, "Blessed is he who comes in the name of the Lord"; grant that with grateful hearts we too may join in the songs of praise of those in heaven and earth who rejoice at Your coming; through Jesus Christ, Your Son, our Lord. Amen. (1)

### ❧ *Christmas Eve*

O God, because You once caused this holy night to shine with the brightness of the true Light, grant that we who have known the mystery of that Light here on earth may come to the full measure of its joys in heaven; through Jesus Christ, Your Son, our Lord. Amen. (2)

### ❧ *Christmas Day*

Grant, almighty God, that the birth of Your only-begotten Son in human flesh may set us free, who in sin are held in bondage; through Jesus Christ, Your Son, our Lord. Amen. (3)

### ❧ *Epiphany*

O God, by the leading of a star You once made known to all nations Your only-begotten Son; now lead us, who know You by faith, to know in heaven the fullness of Your divine goodness; through Jesus Christ, Your Son, our Lord. Amen. (4)

### ❧Lent

Almighty and everlasting God, because You hate nothing You have made and forgive the sins of all who are penitent, create in us new and contrite hearts that we, worthily repenting our sins and acknowledging our wretchedness, may obtain from You, the God of all mercy, perfect remission and forgiveness; through Jesus Christ, Your Son, our Lord. Amen. (5)

### ❧Palm Sunday

Almighty and everlasting God the Father, who sent Your Son to take our nature upon Him and to suffer death on the cross that all mankind should follow the example of His great humility, mercifully grant that we may both follow the example of our Savior Jesus Christ in His patience and also have our portion in His resurrection; through Jesus Christ, Your Son, our Lord. Amen. (6)

### ❧Good Friday

Merciful and everlasting God, the Father, who did not spare Your only Son, but delivered Him up for us all that He might bear our sins on the cross, grant that our hearts may be so fixed with steadfast faith in our Savior that we may not fear the power of any adversaries; through Jesus Christ, Your Son, our Lord. Amen. (7)

### ❧ Easter

O God, for our redemption You have given Your only-begotten Son to the death of the cross, and by His glorious resurrection You have delivered us from the power of our enemy. Therefore grant that all our sins may be drowned through daily repentance and that day by day a new man may arise to live before You in righteousness and purity forever; through Jesus Christ, Your Son, our Lord. Amen. (8)

### ❧ For Pentecost

O God, on this day You once taught the hearts of Your faithful people by sending them the light of Your Holy Spirit. Grant us in our day by the same Spirit to have a right understanding in all things and evermore to rejoice in His holy consolation; through Jesus Christ, Your Son, our Lord. Amen. (9)

### ❧ For Trinity

Almighty and everlasting God, since You have given us, Your servants, grace to acknowledge the glory of the eternal Trinity by the confession of a true faith, and to worship the true Unity in the power of Your divine majesty, keep us also steadfast in this true faith and worship, and defend us ever from all our adversaries; through

Jesus Christ, Your Son, our Lord. Amen. (10)

### ❦ *For Reformation*

Almighty God, gracious Lord, pour out Your Holy Spirit on Your faithful people. Keep them steadfast in Your grace and truth, protect and comfort them in all temptations, defend them against all enemies of Your Word, and bestow on the Church Your saving peace; through Jesus Christ, Your Son, our Lord. Amen. (11)

## 2.

## The Church and the Kingdom of God

### ❦ *General Prayer*

O God almighty and merciful, let Your fatherly kindness be upon all whom You have made; hear the prayers of all who call upon You; open the eyes of those who never pray for themselves; pity the sighs of such as are in misery; deal mercifully with those who are in darkness; increase the number and graces of those who fear and serve You daily; preserve this land from the misfortunes of war, this church from all wild and dangerous errors, this people from forgetting You, their Lord and Benefactor; be gracious to all those countries that are made desolate by earthquakes, droughts, floods, epidemics, or persecution; bless all persons and places to which Your providence has made us debtors, all who have been instrumental to our good by their assistance, advice, example, or writings, and make us in our turn useful to others; let none of those who desire our prayers want for Your mercy, but defend and comfort and conduct them through to their life's end; through Jesus Christ, Your Son, our Lord. Amen. (12)

### ¶Confession and Deliverance

Almighty and merciful God, the Fountain of all goodness, who knows the thoughts of my heart, I confess unto You that I have sinned against You and am evil in your sight; wash me I implore You from the stains of my past sins, and give me grace and power to put away all hurtful things, so that, being delivered from the bondage of sin, I may bring forth worthy fruits of repentance; O Eternal Light, shine into my heart; O Eternal Goodness, deliver me from evil; O Eternal Power, be to me a support; eternal Wisdom, scatter the darkness of my ignorance; eternal Pity, have mercy upon me; grant unto me that with all my heart and mind and strength I may evermore seek Your face; and finally bring me in Your infinite mercy to Your holy presence; so strengthen my weakness that, following in the footsteps of Your blessed Son, I may obtain the promise of my Baptism and enter into Your promised joy; through the same Jesus Christ, Your Son, our Lord. Amen. (13)

### ❧ For the Church

O God, our heavenly Father, who manifested Your love by sending Your only-begotten Son into the world that all might live through Him, pour Your Holy Spirit upon Your church that it may fulfill His command to preach the Gospel in every land; send forth, we implore You, laborers into Your harvest; defend them in all dangers and temptations and hasten the time when they and those whom they have brought to You will meet and rejoice before Your heavenly throne; through Jesus Christ, Your Son, our Lord. Amen. (14)

### ❧ The Litany

*When used in group settings, the responses are set in* **bold type.**

O Lord, **have mercy.** O Christ, **have mercy.** O Lord, **have mercy.** O Christ, **hear us.** God the Father, in heaven, **have mercy.** God the Son, Redeemer of the world, **have mercy.** God the Holy Spirit, **have mercy.** Be gracious to us. **Spare us, good Lord.** Be gracious to us. **Help us, good Lord.**

From all sin, from all error, from all evil: from the crafts and assaults of the devil; from sudden and evil death: from pestilence and famine; from war and bloodshed; from sedition and from rebellion: from lightning and tempest; from all calamity by fire and water; and from everlasting death: **Good Lord, deliver us.**

By the mystery of Your holy incarnation; by Your holy nativity: by Your baptism, fasting, and temptation; by Your agony and bloody sweat; by Your cross and Passion; by Your precious death and burial: by Your glorious resurrection and ascension; and by the coming of the Holy Spirit, the Comforter: **Help us, good Lord.**

In all time of our tribulation; in all time of our prosperity; in the hour of death; and in the day of judgment: **Help us, good Lord.** We poor sinners implore You to **hear us, O Lord.**

To rule and govern Your holy Christian Church; to preserve all pastors and ministers of Your Church in the true knowledge and understanding of Your wholesome Word and to sustain them in holy living: to put an end to all schisms and causes of offense; to bring into the way of truth all who have erred and are deceived: to beat down Satan under our feet; to send faithful laborers into Your harvest; and to accompany Your Word with Your grace and Spirit: **We implore You to hear us, good Lord.**

To raise those that fall and to strengthen those that stand; and to comfort and help the weakhearted and the distressed: **We implore You to hear us, good Lord.** To give to all peoples concord and peace; to preserve our land from discord and strife; to give our country Your protection in every time of need: to direct and defend our president and all in authority; to bless and protect our magistrates and all our people: to watch over and help all who are in danger, necessity, and tribulation; to protect and guide all who travel: to grant all women with child, and all mothers with infant children, increasing happiness in their blessings; to defend all orphans and widows and provide for them: to strengthen and keep all sick persons and young children; to free those in bondage; and to have mercy on us all: **We implore You to hear us, good Lord.**

To forgive our enemies, persecutors, and slanderers and to turn their hearts; to give and preserve to our use the kindly fruits of the earth; and graciously to hear our prayers: **We implore You to hear us, good Lord.** Lord Jesus Christ, Son of God, **we implore You to hear us.**

Christ, the Lamb of God, who takes away the sin of the world, **have mercy.** Christ, the Lamb of God, who takes away the sin of the world, **have mercy.** Christ, the Lamb of God, who takes away the sin of the world, **grant us Your peace.** O Christ, **hear us.** O Lord, **have mercy.** O Christ, **have mercy.** O Lord, **have mercy. Amen.** (15)

### ⁊*For the Non-Christian*

O God of all the nations of the earth, remember the multitudes of non-Christians, who, though created in Your image, are perishing in their sin; and grant that by the prayers and labors of Your holy church they may be delivered from all superstitions and unbelief and brought to worship You; through Him whom you have sent to be our Salvation, the Resurrection and the Life of all the faithful, Your Son, Jesus Christ, our Lord. Amen. (16)

## ¶At the Opening of Church or Church Group Meeting

Lord Jesus Christ, during Your ministry on earth You called disciples to follow You. You have experienced the temptations and dangers of earthly leadership. You know the disappointments and fears that trouble those who seek to serve the Father. By Your perfect life and death You have earned for us the right to be heard and helped. We pray for what we need at this meeting in order to carry out the Father's will. Share the power of Your resurrection with us, that in newness of life we may serve others. Give us perspective and awareness of what You desire for us to do. Keep us from self-centeredness and pettiness in our dealings with others. Forgive us when we fail. Guide Your church in this place, through us and for Your name's sake. Amen. (17)

God, You are the Creator, Redeemer, and Sanctifier. We meet You as you come to us in Word and Sacrament, as You come to us in grace and blessing. We thank You for calling us into Your kingdom. We thank You for allowing us to be members of this congregation. We thank You for appointing us as workers with the saints in this church body. We need Your power to work effectively and to overcome the forces of evil that frustrate Your saving intentions. We seek Your grace, to care for people as You do and to endure hostility and misunderstanding in our efforts to help. We ask that Your holiness fill our lives. Overcome in us the temptation to adopt the ways of the world for the work of Your kingdom in order to enjoy some success. You justify us by Your grace; now sanctify us also according to your great mercy. In Christ, our Lord. Amen. (18)

## 3.

## For Our Neighbors and Ourselves

### ❧ *For Forgiveness*

Grant, merciful Lord, to Your faithful people pardon and peace, that having been set free from our bondage to sin, we may serve You with a quiet mind; through Jesus Christ, Your Son, our Lord, Amen. (19)

### ❧ *For Mercy*

Almighty and everlasting God, always more ready to hear than we to pray and always ready to give more than we either desire or deserve, pour down upon us the abundance of Your mercy, forgiving us those things of which our conscience is afraid, and giving us those good things we are not worthy to ask but through the merits and mediation of Jesus Christ, Your Son, our Lord. Amen. (20)

### ❧ Salvation

O Lord Jesus Christ, Son of the living God, who at the sixth hour was lifted up on the cross for the redemption of the world and shed Your blood for the remission of our sins, grant that by the virtue and merit of Your most holy life, passion, and death we may enter into the gates of paradise with joy; for Your mercy's sake. Amen. (21)

### ❧ For Protection

Almighty God, because You know that we are set among so many and great dangers that by reason of the weakness of our fallen nature we cannot always stand upright, grant us Your strength and protection to support us in all dangers and carry us through all temptations; through Jesus Christ, Your Son, our Lord. Amen. (22)

### ❧ For the Future

O God, You make the minds of Your faithful to be of one will; therefore grant to Your people that they may love what You command and desire what You promise, that among the manifold changes of this age our hearts may ever be fixed where true joys are to be found; through Jesus Christ, Your Son, our Lord. Amen. (23)

### ❧ For Our Enemies

O almighty, everlasting God, through Your own Son, our blessed Lord, You have commanded us to love our enemies, to do good to those who hate us, and to pray for those who persecute us. We pray that by Your gracious visitation all our enemies may be led to true repentance and may have the same love and be of one accord and one mind and heart with us, and with Your whole Church; through Jesus Christ, Your Son, our Lord. Amen. (24)

### ❧ For an Erring Child

Lord Jesus, You came into the world to seek and to save those that were separated from Your love. It is with a heavy and aching heart that I come to You, the Savior of sinners, imploring You to restore to saving faith, my erring child. O Lord, my heart is breaking as I realize that my son (daughter) is following the way of unrepentant sinners, which always leads to condemnation. Save him (her), O Lord, save him (her). You have, in Your vast mercy performed many wonders and I pray that You would lead back all the erring lambs who have wandered away from Your fold.

O Lord, if by any fault or neglect of my own I have caused him (her) to stray from You, I beg of

Your mercy that You would forgive me. Guide me by Your Holy Word and show me how to share Your love, mercy, and forgiveness. Draw all of us closer to You in faith. If it be Your will, let this erring child be returned so our hearts are filled again with Your peace and Your joy. Unite us with You in faith and abide in our hearts both now and forevermore as our loving, compassionate, and forgiving Savior. In Your holy name I pray. Amen. (25)

### ❧ For Those Who Have Forsaken the Faith

Almighty, merciful, and gracious God and Father, visit those who have forsaken the Christian faith and those who wandered from Your Word; reveal to them their error and bring them back from their wanderings, that they with singleness of heart, and taking pleasure in the pure truth of Your Word alone, may be made partakers of eternal life; through Jesus Christ, Your Son, our Lord. Amen. (26)

### ❧ For Peace

Almighty and most merciful God, You bring us through suffering and death with our Lord Jesus Christ to enter with Him into eternal glory. Grant us grace at all times to acknowledge and accept Your holy and gracious will, to remain in true faith, and to find peace and joy in the resurrection of the dead, and of the glory of everlasting life; through Jesus Christ, Your Son, our Lord. Amen. (27)

### ¶In Time of War

Father of mercies and God of all comfort, look in pity upon all who are suffering in this time of strife and the warfare of nations. Protect the defenseless, heal the wounded, console the anxious and bereaved, and receive to Yourself those who die in the Lord Jesus Christ. Turn the hearts of our enemies, we pray, and forgive both them and us for our share in the sin that has brought this anguish upon humankind. Open up to us a way of reconciliation and lead us into the path of peace; through Jesus Christ, Your Son, our Lord. Amen. (28)

### ¶For the Nation

O God, our Refuge and Strength, who orders all things in heaven and earth, look upon this nation with Your mercy; remember not our iniquities or the iniquities of our forefathers, and do not take Your just vengeance for our sins; pour out on us and on all the people of this land the spirit of grace and supplication and join us together in piety, loyalty, and brotherly love; direct the counsels and strengthen the hands of all in authority for the repression of crime and violence, the maintenance of order and law and of public peace and safety; so that, leading quiet lives in all godliness and honesty, we may live to be Your people, and You may show Yourself to be our God and that we may bless and glorify you,

our Defender and Deliverer; through Jesus Christ,
Your Son, our Lord, Amen. (29)

### ❧ Christian Life

Direct us, O Lord, in all our actions by Your
gracious favor, and further us with Your continual help that in all our works, begun, continued,
and ended in Your name, we may glorify Your
holy name and finally by Your mercy receive eternal life; through Jesus Christ, Your Son, our Lord.
Amen. (30)

### ❧ Against Temptation and Sin

Grant, O Lord, that when we are tempted, we
may resist the devil; when we are worried, we
may cast all our care upon You; when we are
weary, we may seek Your rest; and in all things we
may live this day to Your glory; through Jesus
Christ, your Son, our Lord. Amen. (31)

Almighty God, since You know we are set in
the midst of so many and great dangers that by
reason of the frailty of our nature we cannot
always stand upright, grant us such strength and
protection as may support us in all dangers and
carry us through all temptations; through Jesus
Christ, Your Son, our Lord. Amen. (32)

### ❧ For Courage

Lord God, You have called Your servants to
ventures of which we cannot see the ending, by

paths as yet untrodden, through perils unknown. Give us faith to go out with good courage, not knowing where we go but only that Your hand is leading us and Your love supporting us; through Jesus Christ, Your Son, our Lord. Amen. (33)

## ❧Prayer of Luther on Casting All Our Cares upon the Lord

Heavenly Father, You are truly my Lord and my God; You have created me, bringing me out of nothing, and You have redeemed me through Your Son. You have appointed and assigned to me this office—this place in life—and all these duties, but matters do not always take the turn I should like them to take, and there are so many things troubling and distressing me that in myself I find neither hope or consolation. For this very reason I commit everything to You, looking to You for counsel and aid. In all these questions be the Beginning and the End. Amen. (34)

## ❧Of One Seeking a Wife

O you almighty, eternal God, Creator, Preserver and Multiplier of the human race, You instituted marriage while Adam and Eve still dwelt in paradise. You also honored holy matrimony by the first miracle performed by your dear Son, Jesus Christ, our Savior, at the wedding in Cana of Galilee. You know my heart; you know my disposition and attributes, and You know weaknesses and strengths better than I myself.

From You one also receives the gift of a good spouse because that comes alone from the Most High. I beseech you from the heart that You would grant me a good, Christian, God-fearing wife whom I would ever hold dear in my heart. I pray that this companion and I might peacefully and harmoniously live upon earth in the true fear of God and in this Christian journey. I cry to you, make my heart fit regarding such things, and enlighten me with your Holy Spirit. And having commended the matter to Your fatherly care, let me be at peace; for the sake of Jesus Christ. Amen. (35)

### ᐁ *A Single Man's Prayer*

Merciful Father, You have promised to sustain us, Your children, throughout our earthly pilgrimage, whatever it may be that You have planned. St. Paul, as a single person, lived out his entire earthly pilgrimage willingly with graciousness and thanksgiving. I fervently pray that You will sustain me with the same spirit. Grant me the willingness to accept my vocation as a single person and grant me sustenance through the Body of Christ. Continue to surround me with family and friends and grant me the opportunity to serve You and Your church. Finally, grant me the ability to live out my earthly pilgrimage with contentment and joy. Amen. (36)

### ¶A Husband's Prayer

Almighty God, You created marriage as the union of husband and wife in body and soul, so that each can be a help, comfort and joy to the other in times of prosperity and good health as well as in times of adversity and suffering. I praise You for the blessings You bestow on me through my wife. During our life together you have accompanied us with your constant mercy and loving-kindness. In sorrow and sickness you have strengthened us. From temptation to infidelity and divorce you have delivered us. As you have forgiven all our sins because of the merits of our crucified and risen Lord Jesus Christ, you have enabled us to forgive one another. Trusting in Your grace alone, I implore you to preserve us in faith and grant us continuing wedded joy. Amen. (37)

### ¶Husband's Prayer at Childbirth

O God, our Father, the creator of life and bringer of joy, I pray on behalf of my wife who is now in the pains and anguish of labor. Shorten her suffering, increase her patience, and do not lay upon her more than You will enable her to bear. In Your good time send her ease and cause her to be delivered. Preserve the infant that now struggles for its birth; and as it be Your will speedily place into her arms a hopeful child, that together as a family we may live in the faith which gives us eternal life in Your Son, our Lord Jesus Christ. Amen. (38)

### ❧ Father's Thanksgiving after Childbirth

O God, Creator of Life, you have again revealed Yourself in the beautiful miracle of birth; thank you for alleviating my wife's pain and for holding Your protecting hand over her during delivery. Thank you for your mercy; it was Your power that preserved her, Your goodness that delivered her, Your hand that supported us both.

You have lent us this precious child for our comfort and joy; give us grace to cherish him/her. Take us and this child into Your tender mercy and keep us always safe with You. Defend him/her from all dangers of body and soul, delivering him/her safely to the waters of his/her baptism where he/she will receive the righteousness of Your Son, Jesus, and become Your beloved child; through Jesus Christ. Amen. (39)

### ❧ Of a Widower

Father of mercy and God of all comfort, my only help in all my need, You give and take away according to Your wisdom. You bring down the proud and raise up those whom You have humbled. I cry to You now out of the depths of my sadness, with groans of misery too deep for words, because, through temporal death, You have taken from my side the dear woman whom You gave to be with me. My loss is great, for she has been the delight of my eyes, my true companion, the glory of my house, in whom my heart could safely trust regarding all that concerns my earthly welfare.

Lord, look upon my tears, consider my agony of heart and mind and soul, and forgive me all my sin. Do not leave me in despair. You have said, "it is not good that the man should be alone" (Genesis 2:18), yet I am now bereft of my helpmate; I am alone and miserable. Comfort me with Your gracious presence, for the fear in my heart is great. Therefore, teach me by Your Spirit through Word and Sacrament that You are with me and have not left me without consolation.

I confess that, as a husband, I have been a poor reflection of that dear Savior, Jesus Christ. But do not allow my failings to give the devil any foothold in my life. I pray to You in all humility, in repentance and with faith in Your forgiveness: prevent me from becoming lost in my misery. Nor let me falter, in my grief, in those other vocations and responsibilities that remain to me. Enable me to serve my family and neighbor faithfully, even as You continue to serve and protect me. Into Your hands, O Lord, I commend myself entirely; let me never come to ruin. Be my Comfort, my Shield and Strength, my Fortress and strong Tower, my Help and constant Companion, that I may praise You for Your faithfulness unto all eternity; through Christ, my Lord. Amen. (40)

### ❧ For House/Home

Bless, O Lord, this house and all who dwell in it, as You were pleased to bless the house of Abraham, Isaac, and Jacob, that within these walls may dwell an angel of light and that we who dwell together in it may receive the abundant dew of heavenly blessing and through Your tender mercy rejoice in peace and quietness; through Jesus Christ, Your Son, our Lord. Amen. (41)

### ❧ Before Travel

Lord God our Father, You kept Abraham and Sarah in safety throughout the days of their pilgrimage, You led the children of Israel through the midst of the sea, and by a star You led the Wise Men to the infant Jesus. Protect and guide us now in this time as we set out to travel, make our ways safe and our homecomings joyful, and bring us at last to our heavenly home; through Jesus Christ, Your Son, our Lord. Amen. (42)

### ❧ Strife in the Home

Father of all who blesses us beyond measure, You placed us together that we might be a help to each other, that we would support and strengthen the other not only for the trials of this life, but also in faith and for the life to come. Have mercy on us; for I have not lived my life according to Your will and by choosing my will over Yours, I have brought strife into my home.

O God, You know how prone my heart is to mistrust, temper, lack of patience and strife. Forgive me for praying so little, for my want of love, for stubbornly insisting on my rights and my own way. Come to us and help us. Make us to know again that without Your peace our hearts will have no peace. Give us, O God, the will and the means to be reconciled to You and to one another; join us to Yourself through Word and Sacrament that we may live together and with You in the peace that only You can give; through Your Son, our Lord Jesus Christ. Amen. (43)

### ❧ Prayer of an Elderly Man

Lord God, our continual Refuge, our life in old age, in whose hands our time abides: Look! The years are come upon me, of which I would say: they do not please me. For my abilities in this advanced age are continually being taken from me, and all about me, difficulties and weaknesses have increased in number. You have so graciously and fatherly cared for me from the time that I was in the womb; from my youth, you have remained my Hope. I pray that you will not depart from me in my old age, in which I have grown gray and weak, but until my life's blessed end lift up, bear and save me. Especially I pray to you, O gracious Father, that you would govern and lead me with your Holy Spirit, that I may wholly dedicate the rest of my time on earth to be with you on a Christian pilgrimage, with you in prayer and sighing and remain evermore in Christian preparation for a blessed end. May I be ready, so that if today or tomorrow my life should reach its goal, I may with old Simeon in peace depart this world unto life eternal. Amen. (44)

### ❧ For Joy in My Job

Heavenly Father, creator of heaven and earth, it is out of Your love and wisdom that You gave me work to do, and fitted me in body and mind to do this work. And yet my sinful will too often dreads the workday and casts about for other things to do. But You, O God, have called me to this work. Forgive me my sin. Strengthen me by Your Spirit that I may see that my place of work is a field of Your service to my family, my fellow worker, and to my neighbor. Give me joy in my vocation and make me glad and grateful for the strength to serve You; through Jesus Christ. Amen. (45)

### ❧ Prayer of Comfort Concerning Vocation

Dear Lord, I have your Word and I am in the path of life that pleases you, this I know. Yet I look around and see how everywhere there is a lack of answers, a lack of help, and a lack of that which I need now! I can turn to no one for help except to You. Help me with all of this. My comfort is in this: You have said and commanded that I should ask, search and knock, and so doing I will certainly receive, find, and have that which I desire. Amen. (46)

### ¶ Of a Businessman

Lord, You have prospered the labor of my hands and have given success to my undertakings. Oh, kind and gracious Father, grant me always a grateful heart, that I may never forget how completely unworthy I am in all the mercies and of all the truth which you have shown your servant. Grant me a lively sense of my responsibilities and obligations, which You have placed upon me. Deeply impress upon me the need of remaining humble, of trusting not in wealth or material goods but in You, the living God, and in Your Son, my only Savior. Keep me mindful that You, who have so richly given me all things to enjoy, can quickly take away all that I have. Teach me, O God of love, to be rich in good works, always ready to help my brothers and sisters, ever willing to contribute, according to my ability, toward the building up of Your kingdom both here and abroad. By the power of Your Spirit, help me to store up treasure not merely upon this earth, but especially in heaven, which Christ has procured for me by the payment of His precious blood. Amen. (47)

### ❧ *Thanksgiving upon Completion of Work*

Almighty, eternal, and gracious God, I give You hearty thanks and praise for Your most holy aid and assistance shown me this day. Without You I surely could have done nothing, and therefore all praise belongs to You. I pray, be pleased with my work, and have it tend to the welfare, in body and soul, of myself and my fellow man; through Jesus Christ, our Lord. Amen. (48)

### ❧ *For the Family During Unemployment*

Heavenly Father I come to You for aid and encouragement during these days of unemployment. Give to us a fuller measure of faith in the promises of Your Word. Grant that I may live trustingly one day at a time, knowing that You will not fail me. Even the little we receive I accept with a grateful heart. Protect us from the dangers of enforced idleness, unnecessary worry, and sleepless nights. Restore to this family the provision and means to find regular employment. Root out greed, selfishness, and all other distress in our family. Grant us success, earnestness, sobriety, and skill as we seek out work. Heavenly Father, You bless a person through the labor of his hands, satisfy our hunger with bread, and comfort our souls with the peace that comes only from our relationship with You; through Jesus our Lord. Amen. (49)

### ⸸ At Times of Personal Unemployment

O God, You have been my Help in past days, and in the same way I ask You not to turn away from me in this present day as I walk the streets, discouraged and disheartened, seeking work. Lead me and direct me to find suitable work.

O Lord, my sins are ever before me. In my yesterdays I have not always served You; too often I have ignored Your goodness and Your mercy. Forgive me, and let me find peace for my soul in You. Take all resentment, bitterness, and rebellion out of my heart and spirit. Make me hopeful, cheerful, courageous, patient, and confident.

You have promised to be with me in the day of trouble. Open Your hands and satisfy my needs. Teach me to face the day confident of Your goodness. O Lord, let me not doubt Your promises. Hear the cry of my distressed heart and disturbed mind. Have mercy upon me, for Jesus' sake. Amen. (50)

### ⸸ For the Sick

Almighty God, who forgives all our iniquities and heals all our diseases, who has proclaimed Your name to be the Lord that heals us and has sent Your beloved Son to bear our sicknesses, look in mercy upon Your unworthy servants, pardon and forgive our transgressions, and of Your loving-kindness remove the plague of sickness with which You have visited us. This we ask according to Your will through Jesus Christ, our Lord. Amen. (51)

### ❧ During Personal Illness

Divine Lord, You have been gracious and merciful to me in Christ Jesus. Forgive me all my sins day after day. Accept my thanks for this Your goodness. Let me find my joy in You who have brought to my heart salvation and peace.

In Your mercy look upon my distress and pain, and forgive me all my sins and all my worry. Ease my sufferings, and make me patient and cheerful in my affliction. Bless those who take care of me. Let them not become weary in this service that they must render to me. Keep me faithful to Your Word, and grant that I may continue in Your grace until life's journey ends and I behold You in the glory of eternity, through Jesus Christ, our Lord. Amen. (52)

### ❧ When Recovery Is Slow

O God, the Father of our Lord Jesus Christ, in whose grace we find the strength and patience to endure; You have relieved us in our distress and You have brought us this far in our recovery—in many ways You have shown Your loving-kindness to us day by day. Help us now to follow You to the end giving us the strength and peace to conquer hopeless brooding and irritable impatience.

Continue to bless those who you have placed before us with the means to effect our recovery. Do not let sickness distract us or weaken our service to our neighbor. As it is your will, lay no more upon us than You will enable us to bear, but with strength and resolution enable us to bear this cross for the time it has been appointed to us.

In all our days of despair give the grace to recall Your past mercies, that in faith we may be encouraged. Strengthen our faith and confirm our hope that we may never openly complain or secretly murmur against You, but that even in our trouble we may be a witness to Your merciful care. Confirm in us the hope that by Your grace you will deliver us from our troubles or You will sanctify them and make them work together for our good. Through Jesus Christ our Lord. Amen. (53)

### ❧As Death Approaches

Depart in peace, you ransomed soul. May God the Father almighty who created you; may God the Son who redeemed you with His blood; may God the Holy Spirit who sanctified you in the water of Holy Baptism, receive you into the company of the saints and angels who live in the light of His glory forevermore; through Jesus Christ, Your Son, our Lord. Amen. (54)

O Lord, one whom I love and care about is dying. Yet Your love of him (her) is still greater for

You have redeemed him (her) with the precious blood of Your Son. If it be Your will that he (she) should pass out of this mortal life, receive him (her) to Yourself in glory. If this be his (her) last night on earth, let Your holy angels take him (her) into Your presence, where there is no more pain and suffering and sin, but fullness of joy forevermore. Wash him (her) of all sin, and accept him (her) for Jesus' sake. Strengthen our faith, and keep us close to You. In Jesus' name we ask it. Amen. (55)

### ❧ After a Death

Amid my tears, O Lord, I praise You as You have received (<u>name</u>) to Yourself in glory for all eternity. I thank You that You have brought him (her) to the knowledge of Jesus Christ, our Lord and Savior. Comfort all who mourn with the glorious hope of the resurrection and life eternal. Grant me grace to say with a believing heart: "Thy will be done," and to know Your will is a good and gracious will even in the present hour. Comfort me through Your Gospel, which promises strength and help to the troubled and weary. O Lord, forsake me not in this hour. Prepare me through Your Word and Sacrament for that day when You will call me to Yourself that I may joyfully join the whole company of heaven to live with You forever; for Jesus' sake I ask it. Amen. (56)

# A Brief Summary of the Christian Faith

*This is the text of Dr. Martin Luther's Small Catechism, the most popular explanation of the central teachings of the Christian faith. It has been used by countless Christians of all denominations for almost 500 years.*

## The Ten Commandments

*As the head of the family should teach them in a simple way to his household*

### The First Commandment

**You shall have no other gods.**

*What does this mean?* We should fear, love, and trust in God above all things.

### The Second Commandment

**You shall not misuse the name of the Lord your God.**

*What does this mean?* We should fear and love God so that we do not curse, swear, use satanic arts, lie, or deceive by His name, but call upon it in every trouble, pray, praise, and give thanks.

### The Third Commandment

**Remember the Sabbath day**

**by keeping it holy.**

*What does this mean?* We should fear and love God so that we do not despise preaching and His Word, but hold it sacred and gladly hear and learn it.

## The Fourth Commandment

**Honor your father and your mother.**

*What does this mean?* We should fear and love God so that we do not despise or anger our parents and other authorities, but honor them, serve and obey them, love and cherish them.

## The Fifth Commandment

**You shall not murder.**

*What does this mean?* We should fear and love God so that we do not hurt or harm our neighbor in his body, but help and support him in every physical need.

## The Sixth Commandment

**You shall not commit adultery.**

*What does this mean?* We should fear and love God so that we lead a sexually pure and decent life in what we say and do, and husband and wife love and honor each other.

## The Seventh Commandment

**You shall not steal.**

*What does this mean?* We should fear and love God so that we do not take our neighbor's money or possessions, or get them in any dishonest way, but help him to improve and protect his possessions and income.

## The Eighth Commandment

**You shall not give false testimony against your neighbor.**

*What does this mean?* We should fear and love God so that we do not tell lies about our neighbor, betray him, slander him, or hurt his reputation, but defend him, speak well of him, and explain everything in the kindest way.

## The Ninth Commandment

**You shall not covet your neighbor's house.**

*What does this mean?* We should fear and love God so that we do not scheme to get our neighbor's inheritance or house, or get it in a way which only appears right, but help and be of service to him in keeping it.

## The Tenth Commandment

**You shall not covet your neighbor's wife, or his manservant or maidservant, his ox or donkey, or anything that belongs to your neighbor.**

*What does this mean?* We should fear and love God so that we do not entice or force away our neighbor's wife, workers, or animals, or turn them against him, but urge them to stay and do their duty.

[The text of the commandments is from Exodus 20:3, 7–8, 12–17.]

## The Close of the Commandments

*What does God say about all these commandments?*

He says: "I, the Lord your God, am a jealous God, punishing the children for the sin of the fathers to the third and fourth generation of those who hate Me, but showing love to a thousand generations of those who love Me and keep My commandments." *[Exodus 20:5–6]*

*What does this mean?* God threatens to punish all who break these commandments. Therefore, we should fear His wrath and not do anything against them. But He promises grace and every blessing to all who keep these commandments. Therefore, we should also love and trust in Him and gladly do what He commands.

# The Creed

*As the head of the family should teach it in a simple way to his household*

### The First Article

## Creation

I believe in God, the Father Almighty, Maker of heaven and earth.

*What does this mean?* I believe that God has made me and all creatures; that He has given me my body and soul, eyes, ears, and all my members, my reason and all my senses, and still takes care of them.

He also gives me clothing and shoes, food and drink, house and home, wife and children, land, animals, and all I have. He richly and daily provides me with all that I need to support this body and life.

He defends me against all danger and guards and protects me from all evil.

All this He does only out of fatherly, divine goodness and mercy, without any merit or worthiness in me. For all this it is my duty to thank and praise, to serve and obey Him.

This is most certainly true.

**The Second Article**

## Redemption

**And in Jesus Christ, His only Son, our Lord, who was conceived by the Holy Spirit, born of the Virgin Mary, suffered under Pontius Pilate, was crucified, died and was buried. He descended into hell. The third day He rose again from the dead. He ascended into heaven and sits at the right hand of God the Father Almighty. From thence He will come to judge**

**the living and the dead.**

*What does this mean?* I believe that Jesus Christ, true God, begotten of the Father from eternity, and also true man, born of the Virgin Mary, is my Lord, who has redeemed me, a lost and condemned person, purchased and won me from all sins, from death, and from the power of the devil; not with gold or silver, but with His holy, precious blood and with His innocent suffering and death, that I may be His own and live under Him in His kingdom, and serve Him in everlasting righteousness, innocence, and blessedness, just as He is risen from the dead, lives and reigns to all eternity.

This is most certainly true.

### The Third Article

## Sanctification

**I believe in the Holy Spirit, the holy Christian Church, the communion of saints, the forgiveness of sins, the resurrection of the body, and the life everlasting. Amen**

*What does this mean?* I believe that I cannot by my own reason or strength believe in Jesus Christ, my Lord, or come to Him; but the Holy Spirit has called me by the Gospel, enlightened me with His gifts, sanctified and kept me in the true faith.

In the same way He calls, gathers, enlightens, and sanctifies the whole Christian Church on earth and keeps it with Jesus Christ in the one true faith.

In this Christian Church He daily and richly forgives all my sins and the sins of all believers.

On the Last Day He will raise me and all the dead, and give eternal life to me and all believers in Christ.

This is most certainly true.

## The Lord's Prayer

*As the head of the family should teach it in a simple way to his household*

**Our Father, who art in heaven, hallowed be Thy name, Thy kingdom come, Thy will be done on earth as it is in heaven. Give us this day our daily bread; and forgive us our trespasses as we forgive those who trespass against us; and lead us not into temptation, but deliver us from evil. For Thine is the kingdom and the power and the glory forever and ever. Amen.**

### The Introduction

**Our Father who art in heaven.**

*What does this mean?* With these words God tenderly invites us to believe that He is our true Father and that we are His true children, so that with all boldness and confidence we may ask Him as dear children ask their dear father.

## The First Petition

**Hallowed be Thy name.**

*What does this mean?* God's name is certainly holy in itself, but we pray in this petition that it may be kept holy among us also.

*How is God's name kept holy?* God's name is kept holy when the Word of God is taught in its truth and purity, and we, as the children of God, also lead holy lives according to it. Help us to do this, dear Father in heaven! But anyone who teaches or lives contrary to God's Word profanes the name of God among us. Protect us from this, heavenly Father!

## The Second Petition

**Thy kingdom come.**

*What does this mean?* The kingdom of God certainly comes by itself without our prayer, but we pray in this petition that it may come to us also.

*How does God's kingdom come?* God's kingdom comes when our heavenly Father gives us His Holy Spirit, so that by His grace we believe His holy Word and lead godly lives here in time and there in eternity.

## The Third Petition

**Thy will be done on earth as it is in heaven.**

*What does this mean?* The good and gracious will of God is done even without our prayer, but we pray in this petition that it may be done among us also.

*How is God's will done?* God's will is done when He breaks and hinders every evil plan and purpose of the devil, the world, and our sinful nature, which do not want us to hallow God's name or let His kingdom come; and when He strengthens and keeps us firm in His Word and faith until we die.

This is His good and gracious will.

### The Fourth Petition

### Give us this day our daily bread.

*What does this mean?* God certainly gives daily bread to everyone without our prayers, even to all evil people, but we pray in this petition that God would lead us to realize this and to receive our daily bread with thanksgiving.

*What is meant by daily bread?* Daily bread includes everything that has to do with the support and needs of the body, such as food, drink, clothing, shoes, house, home, land, animals, money, goods, a devout husband or wife, devout children, devout workers, devout and faithful rulers, good government, good weather, peace, health, self-control, good reputation, good friends, faithful neighbors, and the like.

## The Fifth Petition

**And forgive us our trespasses as we forgive those who trespass against us.**

*What does this mean?* We pray in this petition that our Father in heaven would not look at our sins, or deny our prayer because of them. We are neither worthy of the things for which we pray, nor have we deserved them, but we ask that He would give them all to us by grace, for we daily sin much and surely deserve nothing but punishment. So we too will sincerely forgive and gladly do good to those who sin against us.

## The Sixth Petition

**And lead us not into temptation.**

*What does this mean?* God tempts no one. We pray in this petition that God would guard and keep us so that the devil, the world, and our sinful nature may not deceive us or mislead us into false belief, despair, and other great shame and vice. Although we are attacked by these things, we pray that we may finally overcome them and win the victory.

## The Seventh Petition

**But deliver us from evil.**

*What does this mean?* We pray in this petition, in summary, that our Father in heaven would rescue us from every evil of body and soul, possessions and reputation, and finally, when our last hour comes, give us a blessed end, and graciously take us from this valley of sorrow to Himself in heaven.

### The Conclusion

**For Thine is the kingdom and the power and the glory forever and ever. Amen.**

*What does this mean?* This means that I should be certain that these petitions are pleasing to our Father in heaven, and are heard by Him; for He Himself has commanded us to pray in this way and has promised to hear us. Amen, amen means "yes, yes, it shall be so."

# The Sacrament of Holy Baptism

*As the head of the family should teach it in a simple way to his household*

### First

*What is Baptism?*

Baptism is not just plain water, but it is the water included in God's command and combined with God's word.

*Which is that word of God?*

Christ our Lord says in the last chapter of Matthew: **"Therefore go and make disciples of all nations, baptizing them in the name of the Father and of the Son and of the Holy Spirit."** [Matthew 28:19]

### Second

*What benefits does Baptism give?*

It works forgiveness of sins, rescues from death and the devil, and gives eternal salvation to all who believe this, as the words and promises of God declare.

*Which are these words and promises of God?*

Christ our Lord says in the last chapter of Mark: **"Whoever believes and is baptized will be saved, but whoever does not believe will be condemned."** *[Mark 16:16]*

### Third

*How can water do such great things?*

Certainly not just water, but the word of God in and with the water does these things, along with the faith which trusts this word of God in the water. For without God's word the water is plain water and no Baptism. But with the word of God it is a Baptism, that is, a life-giving water, rich in grace, and a washing of the new birth in the Holy Spirit, as St. Paul says in Titus chapter three:

**"He saved us through the washing of rebirth and renewal by the Holy Spirit, whom He poured out on us generously through Jesus Christ our Savior, so that, having been justified by His grace, we might become heirs having the hope of eternal life. This is a trustworthy saying."** *[Titus 3:5–8]*

### Fourth

*What does such baptizing with water indicate?*

It indicates that the Old Adam in us should by daily contrition and repentance be drowned and die with all sins and evil desires, and that a new man should daily emerge and arise to live before God in righteousness and purity forever.

*Where is this written?*

St. Paul writes in Romans chapter six: **"We were therefore buried with Him through baptism into death in order that, just as Christ was raised from the dead through the glory of the Father, we too may live a new life."** [Romans 6:4]

# Confession and The Office of the Keys

*How Christians should be taught to confess*

*What is Confession?*

Confession has two parts.

First, that we confess our sins, and second, that we receive absolution, that is, forgiveness, from the pastor as from God Himself, not doubting, but firmly believing that by it our sins are forgiven before God in heaven.

*What sins should we confess?*

Before God we should plead guilty of all sins, even those we are not aware of, as we do in the Lord's Prayer; but before the pastor we should confess only those sins which we know and feel in our hearts.

*Which are these?*

Consider your place in life according to the Ten Commandments: Are you a father, mother, son, daughter, husband, wife, or worker? Have you been disobedient, unfaithful, or lazy? Have you been hot-tempered, rude, or quarrelsome? Have you hurt someone by your words or deeds? Have you stolen, been negligent, wasted anything, or done any harm?

## A Short Form of Confession

[Luther intended the following form to serve only as an example of private confession for Christians of his time.]

*The penitent says:* Dear confessor, I ask you please to hear my confession and to pronounce forgiveness in order to fulfill God's will.

I, a poor sinner, plead guilty before God of all sins. In particular I confess before you that as a servant, maid, etc., I, sad to say, serve my master unfaithfully, for in this and that I have not done what I was told to do. I have hade him angry and caused him to curse. I have been negligent and allowed damage to be done. I have also been offensive in words and deeds. I have quarreled with my peers. I have grumbled about the lady of

175

the house and cursed her. I am sorry for all of this and I ask for grace. I want to do better.

A master or lady of the house may say:

In particular I confess before you that I have not faithfully guided my children, servants, and wife to the glory of God. I have cursed. I have set a bad example by indecent words and deeds. I have hurt my neighbor and spoken evil of him. I have overcharged, sold inferior merchandise, and given less than was paid for.

[Let the penitent confess whatever else he has done against God's commandments and his own position.]

If, however, someone does not find himself burdened with these or greater sins, he should not trouble himself or search for or invent other sins, and thereby make confession a torture. Instead, he should mention one or two that he knows: In particular I confess that I have cursed; I have used improper words; I have neglected this or that, etc. Let that be enough.

But if you know of none at all (which hardly seems possible), then mention none in particular, but receive the forgiveness upon the general confession which you make to God before the confessor.

*Then the confessor shall say:*

God be merciful to you and strengthen your faith. Amen.

*Furthermore:*

Do you believe that my forgiveness is God's forgiveness?

Yes, dear confessor.

*Then let him say:*

Let it be done for you as you believe. And I, by the command of our Lord Jesus Christ, forgive you your sins in the name of the Father and of the Son and of the Holy Spirit. Amen. Go in peace.

A confessor will know additional passages with which to comfort and to strengthen the faith of those who have great burdens of conscience or are sorrowful and distressed.

*This is intended only as a general form of confession.*

*What is the Office of the Keys?*

The Office of the Keys is that special authority which Christ has given to His Church on earth to forgive the sins of repentant sinners, but to withhold forgiveness from the unrepentant as long as they do not repent.

*Where is this written?*

This is what St. John the Evangelist writes in chapter twenty: The Lord Jesus breathed on His disciples and said, **"Receive the Holy Spirit. If you forgive anyone his sins, they are forgiven; if you do not forgive them, they are not forgiven."** *[John 20:22–23]*

*What do you believe according to these words?*

I believe that when the called ministers of Christ deal with us by His divine command, in particular when they exclude openly unrepentant sinners from the Christian congregation and absolve those who repent of their sins and want to do better, this is just as valid and certain, even in heaven, as if Christ our dear Lord dealt with us Himself.

## The Sacrament of the Altar

*As the head of the family should teach it in a simple way to his household*

*What is the Sacrament of the Altar?*

It is the true body and blood of our Lord Jesus Christ under the bread and wine, instituted by Christ Himself for us Christians to eat and to drink.

*Where is this written?*

The holy Evangelists Matthew, Mark, Luke, and St. Paul write:

**Our Lord Jesus Christ, on the night when He was betrayed, took bread, and when He had given thanks, He broke it and gave it to the disciples and said: "Take, eat; this is My body, which is given for you. This do in remembrance of Me."**

**In the same way also He took the cup after**

supper, and when He had given thanks, He gave it to them, saying, "Drink of it, all of you; this cup is the new testament in My blood, which is shed for you for the forgiveness of sins. This do, as often as you drink it, in remembrance of Me."

*What is the benefit of this eating and drinking?*

These words, "Given and shed for you for the forgiveness of sins," show us that in the Sacrament forgiveness of sins, life, and salvation are given us through these words. For where there is forgiveness of sins, there is also life and salvation.

## How can bodily eating and drinking do such great things?

Certainly not just eating and drinking do these things, but the words written here: "Given and shed for you for the forgiveness of sins." These words, along with the bodily eating and drinking, are the main thing in the Sacrament. Whoever believes these words has exactly what they say: "forgiveness of sins."

*Who receives this sacrament worthily?*

Fasting and bodily preparation are certainly fine outward training. But that person is truly worthy and well prepared who has faith in these words: "Given and shed for you for the forgiveness of sins."

179

But anyone who does not believe these words or doubts them is unworthy and unprepared, for the words "for you" require all hearts to believe.

## Daily Prayers

*How the head of the family should teach his household to pray morning and evening*

### Morning Prayer

*In the morning when you get up, make the sign of the holy cross and say:*

In the name of the Father and of the ✠ Son and of the Holy Spirit. Amen.

*Then, kneeling or standing, repeat the Creed and the Lord's Prayer. If you choose, you may also say this little prayer:*

I thank You, my heavenly Father, through Jesus Christ, Your dear Son, that You have kept me this night from all harm and danger; and I pray that You would keep me this day also from sin and every evil, that all my doings and life may please You. For into Your hands I commend myself, my body and soul, and all things. Let Your holy angel be with me, that the evil foe may have no power over me. Amen.

*Then go joyfully to your work, singing a hymn, like that of the Ten Commandments, or whatever your devotion may suggest.*

## Evening Prayer

*In the evening when you go to bed, make the sign of the holy cross and say:*

In the name of the Father and of the ✠ Son and of the Holy Spirit. Amen.

*Then kneeling or standing, repeat the Creed and the Lord's Prayer. If you choose, you may also say this little prayer:*

I thank You, my heavenly Father, through Jesus Christ, Your dear Son, that You have graciously kept me this day; and I pray that You would forgive me all my sins where I have done wrong, and graciously keep me this night. For into Your hands I commend myself, my body and soul, and all things. Let Your holy angel be with me, that the evil foe may have no power over me. Amen.

*Then go to sleep at once and in good cheer.*

---

*How the head of the family should teach his household to ask a blessing and return thanks*

## Asking a Blessing

*The children and the members of the household shall go the table reverently, fold their hands, and say:*

The eyes of all look to You, O Lord, and You

give them their food at the proper time. You open Your hand and satisfy the desires of every living thing. [Psalm 145:15–16]

*Then shall be said the Lord's Prayer and the following:*

Lord God, heavenly Father, bless us and these Your gifts which we receive from Your bountiful goodness, through Jesus Christ, our Lord. Amen.

### Returning Thanks

*Also, after eating, they shall, in like manner, reverently and with folded hands say:*

Give thanks to the Lord, for He is good, His love endures forever. He gives food to every creature. He provides food for the cattle and for the young ravens when they call. His pleasure is not in the strength of the horse, nor His delight in the legs of a man; the Lord delights in those who fear Him, who put their hope in His unfailing love. [Psalm 136:1, 25; 147:9–11]

*Then shall be said the Lord's Prayer and the following:*

We thank You, Lord God, heavenly Father, for all Your benefits, through Jesus Christ, our Lord, who lives and reigns with You and the Holy Spirit forever and ever. Amen.

# Table of Duties

*Certain passages of Scripture for various holy orders and positions, admonishing them about their duties and responsibilities*

### To Bishops, Pastors, and Preachers

The overseer must be above reproach, the husband of but one wife, temperate, self-controlled, respectable, hospitable, able to teach, not given to drunkenness, not violent but gentle, not quarrelsome, not a lover of money. He must manage his own family well and see that his children obey him with proper respect.     *1 Timothy 3:2–4*

He must not be a recent convert, or he may become conceited and fall under the same judgment as the devil.     *1 Timothy 3:6*

He must hold firmly to the trustworthy message as it has been taught, so that he can encourage others by sound doctrine and refute those who oppose it.     *Titus 1:9*

### What the Hearers Owe Their Pastors

The Lord has commanded that those who preach the gospel should receive their living from the gospel.     *1 Corinthians 9:14*

Anyone who receives instruction in the word must share all good things with his instructor. Do not be deceived: God cannot be mocked. A man reaps what he sows.     *Galatians 6:6–7*

The elders who direct the affairs of the church well are worthy of double honor, especially those whose work is preaching and teaching. For the Scripture says, "Do not muzzle the ox while it is treading out the grain," and "The worker deserves his wages." *1 Timothy 5:17–18*

We ask you, brothers, to respect those who work hard among you, who are over you in the Lord and who admonish you. Hold them in the highest regard in love because of their work. Live in peace with each other. *1 Thessalonians 5:12–13*

Obey your leaders and submit to their authority. They keep watch over you as men who must give an account. Obey them so that their work will be a joy, not a burden, for that would be of no advantage to you. *Hebrews 13:17*

**Of Civil Government**

Everyone must submit himself to the governing authorities, for there is no authority except that which God has established. The authorities that exist have been established by God. Consequently, he who rebels against the authority is rebelling against what God has instituted, and those who do so will bring judgment on themselves. For rulers hold no terror for those who do right, but for those who do wrong. Do you want to be free from fear of the one in authority? Then do what is right and he will commend you. For he is God's servant to do you good. But if you do wrong, be afraid, for he does not bear the sword for nothing. He is God's servant, an agent of wrath to bring punishment on the wrongdoer.

*Romans 13:1–4*

## Of Citizens

Give to Caesar what is Caesar's, and to God what is God's. *Matthew 22:21*

It is necessary to submit to the authorities, not only because of possible punishment but also because of conscience. This is also why you pay taxes, for the authorities are God's servants, who give their full time to governing. Give everyone what you owe him: If you owe taxes, pay taxes; if revenue, then revenue; if respect, then respect; if honor, then honor. *Romans 13:5–7*

I urge, then, first of all, that requests, prayers, intercession and thanksgiving be made for everyone—for kings and all those in authority, that we may live peaceful and quiet lives in all godliness and holiness. This is good, and pleases God our Savior. *1 Timothy 2:1–3*

Remind the people to be subject to rulers and authorities, to be obedient, to be ready to do whatever is good. *Titus 3:1*

Submit yourselves for the Lord's sake to every authority instituted among men: whether to the king, as the supreme authority, or to governors, who are sent by him to punish those who do wrong and to commend those who do right.

*1 Peter 2:13–14*

## To Husbands

Husbands, in the same way be considerate as you live with your wives, and treat them with respect as the weaker partner and as heirs with you of the gracious gift of life, so that nothing will hinder your prayers.                              *1 Peter 3:7*

Husbands, love your wives and do not be harsh with them. *Colossians 3:19*

## To Wives

Wives, submit to your husbands as to the Lord.                                     *Ephesians 5:22*

They were submissive to their own husbands, like Sarah, who obeyed Abraham and called him her master. You are her daughters if you do what is right and do not give way to fear.

*1 Peter 3:5–6*

## To Parents

Fathers, do not exasperate your children; instead, bring them up in the training and instruction of the Lord.        *Ephesians 6:4*

## To Children

Children, obey your parents in the Lord, for this is right. "Honor your father and your mother"— which is the first commandment with a promise— "that it may go well with you and that you may enjoy long life on the earth."        *Ephesians 6:1–3*

## To Workers of All Kinds

Slaves, obey your earthly masters with respect and fear, and with sincerity of heart, just as you would obey Christ. Obey them not only to win their favor when their eye is on you, but like slaves of Christ, doing the will of God from your heart. Serve wholeheartedly, as if you were serving the Lord, not men, because you know that the Lord will reward everyone for whatever good he does, whether he is slave or free.

*Ephesians 6:5–8*

## To Employers and Supervisors

Masters, treat your slaves in the same way. Do not threaten them, since you know that he who is both their Master and yours is in heaven, and there is no favoritism with Him. *Ephesians 6:9*

## To Youth

Young men, in the same way be submissive to those who are older. All of you, clothe yourselves with humility toward one another, because, "God opposes the proud but gives grace to the humble." Humble yourselves, therefore, under God's mighty hand, that He may lift you up in due time. *1 Peter 5:5–6*

## To Widows

The widow who is really in need and left all alone puts her hope in God and continues night and day to pray and to ask God for help. But the widow who lives for pleasure is dead even while she lives.                    *1 Timothy 5:5–6*

**To Everyone**

The commandments . . . are summed up in this one rule: "Love your neighbor as yourself."
                    *Romans 13:9*

I urge . . . that requests, prayers, intercession and thanksgiving be made for everyone.
                    *1 Timothy 2:1*

*Let each his lesson learn with care, And all the household well shall fare.*

# Index of Sources